PROLOGUE BY HÉCTOR P. TORRES

THE HOLY ANOINTING

GUILLERMO MALDONADO

PROLOGUE BY HÉCTOR P. TORRES

THE HOLY
ANOINTING

GUILLERMO MALDONADO

Our Mission
Called to bring the supernatural power of God
to this generation.

The Holy Anointing
ISBN: 978-1-59272-038-5
Fourth Edition 2007

Unless otherwise indicated, all Scripture quotations are taken
from the *New King James Version* of the Bible. Scripture
quotations taken from THE AMPLIFIED BIBLE, Copyright ©
1954, 1958, 1962, 1965, 1987 by the Lockman Foundation. All
rights reserved. Used by permission. (www.Lockman.org)

Project Director: Addilena Torres
Cover: Danielle Cruz-Nieri

ERJ Publications
13651 SW 143 Ct., Suite 101, Miami, FL 33186
Tel: (305) 382-3171 - Fax: (305) 675-5770

Category:
The Anointing

Printed in the United States of America

Dedication

I dedicate this book to my loving wife, Ana, and my sons, Bryan and Ronald. You are the greatest treasure God has given me. Thank you for inspiring me to continue in ministry.

Also, I want to thank all of the intercessors and the ERJ Publications team for their endless prayers, for me and this ministry, and for your hard work—your faithfulness to this ministry made this book a reality.

Prologue

Today we find many Christian books written about Jesus. In time, we will discover which of these books, godly people wrote. When we read a book written by someone with a close relationship with the Holy Spirit, the difference is evident. This is such a book; it will surely capture us, as we read it. We cannot really testify about what we have not personally experienced.

You are holding in your hands a highly anointed book; it provides one of the most specific teachings ever developed on the anointing. Its author's life and ministry reflects an extraordinary level of the anointing that goes beyond the usual. Through this book you will experience depths of the anointing that are beyond the norm.

Humility is addressed as one of the most important traits of personal character. The author of this book is the pastor of Florida's largest Hispanic church, and he is the first to acknowledge from the innermost depths of his soul, that he owes it all to the grace of God.

Just as they said about Jesus, "He speaks as one who has authority."

Dr. Ronald E. Short
Apostle-Teacher/ Evangelist-Missionary

Table of Contents

Preface

Throughout my travels in Latin America, Canada and the United States, I have noticed that many nations are experiencing a rise in spiritual awakening. Churches are growing and multiplying exponentially. It is common to find "mega-churches" with thousands of members in many cities throughout the continent. However, in the United States and Canada, it is difficult to find Spanish-speaking churches that are experiencing this type of growth.

Currently, one of the fastest growing churches is "Ministerio International El Rey Jesus" in Miami, Florida, under the leadership of Pastor Guillermo Maldonado. I have ministered several times in that congregation and have noticed at first sight the commitment and surrender from its leaders and volunteers, and their determination to extend the Kingdom of God throughout the city of Miami.

One of the contributing factors contributing to the rapid growth of this congregation is the anointing that is present in this church. Undoubtedly, the leadership team has the adequate training to minister and certainly the anointing upon its mentor, spiritual father and teacher, overflows unto the ministry.

Throughout this valuable book, the author relates his knowledge and the firsthand experience obtained through the growth of his ministry and his intimate relationship with the Holy Spirit and the anointing.

This timely book has arrived at the perfect moment, to help those serious seekers in ministry who have been unable to see the fruit of their labor.

I recommend this book to all pastors that desire to see this type of growth in their congregations. I am confident that if you learn and implement its contents, you will see surprising results in very little time.

Dr. Héctor P. Torres, President
Hispanic International Ministries
Woodland Park, CO USA

Introduction

For many years, we witnessed a great number of leaders in the Body of Christ who were restored and mightily used by God, only to see them fall after a short time in ministry. These leaders did not know how to maintain the anointing in their lives.

The purpose of this book is to provide basic principles for ministering in the anointing. I encourage those believers who the Lord is raising up to recognize its purpose and priceless value. My heart's desire is that you continue to minister and flow in the anointing without ever taking it for granted.

Many ministers know how to follow suggested procedures for the anointing, but they do not truly know how to flow in the Holy Spirit.

Remember, the Holy Spirit is a person, not a thing. The anointing is the manifestation of the Holy Spirit. If we learn to flow in it, we will minister effectively, and see supernatural results.

A leader's personal character serves as the foundation, the pillars and the sustaining building blocks of the anointing. Integrity and an irreproachable character are vital conditions required to effectively minister in the anointing. If someone's character is not refined to model Christ's character, the weight of the anointing will eventually lead to failure of his ministry.

I am certain that as we implement the everlasting principles outlined within this book, God's anointing will be greatly magnified in our lives, and His name will be glorified through His Ministry and Church. We shall see His Kingdom overtake nations; bring hope to the sick, the lost, the forgotten; and millions of lives will be transformed for eternity, as His anointing overflows.

CHAPTER 1

The
Anointing

Total dependency on the Holy Spirit directly influences the anointing of Christian leaders, as it is manifested in their lives. Without this divine anointing, they will not be able to bring forth fruit for the Kingdom of God. The church is in urgent need to snap out of its "religious spirit" and this can only be accomplished through the anointing of the Holy Spirit.

Many Christians talk about the anointing of the Holy Spirit, yet few of them understand what the anointing is. Some mistakenly think that it is a magical, or a physical, sensation.

Most leaders today receive training in academic seminaries through worldly methods that provide high levels of intellectual education, based on man's point of view, but fail to receive the important truth of flowing in the supernatural anointing of God. Sadly, most seminaries only teach concepts, methods and procedures. When these students graduate, they might feel ready, since they learned to prepare sermons, preach, baptize, lead services and increase church growth, but they have yet to experience the Presence of the Holy Spirit, and most important of all, they do not know how to enter into His Presence.

Obviously, it is important to know all these methods, but they are far from sufficient. Academic preparation must go hand in hand with the anointing of God; without it, any amount of study, work and effort will be worthless. When the time comes for Christian leaders to put into practice what they learned, but fail to obtain good results, they will become frustrated because they failed to implement God's Written Word.

"[6]Not by might nor by power, but by My Spirit, saith the LORD of hosts." Zechariah 4.6

Before we define the word "anointing", let us look at what the anointing is "not".

Few people know what it means, but are far from personally knowing it; they have little personal experience of how the anointing operates in their lives.

The anointing is not...

The anointing is not a natural ability, professionalism, spectacular events, or a well-developed preaching. Organizations do not give it away, nor does it result from proficient speech or good education. God's anointing is neither quiet nor loud services, nor religious rituals. None of these things entail or represent God's anointing.

God's anointing flows into those that are genuinely humble before the Lord. Now, let us look at what the anointing really means.

What is the anointing?

The following definitions of words describe the origin or root of each word:

- Balal - to flood; to overflow (especially with oil).

- Dashen - to be overweight; to be especially satisfied; to anoint.

- Mimshach - to anoint with oil.

- Mashaj - to consecrate; to anoint with oil; to anoint.

- Cuwk - to cover over or with oil; to anoint.

- Shemen - A type of liquid oil which often comes in the form of perfume; figuratively speaking, it means riches and prosperity.

Greek words which describe anointing.

- Aleifo - to anoint with oil.

- Encrio - to cover with oil; first to rub inside, then to apply as you rub.

- Epicrio - to cover; to rub over, or on it, with oil.

- Murizo - to apply ointment, perfume or something similar; to anoint the body in preparation for burial.

- Crio - to anoint with oil in order to set apart for something specific; to serve; Holy anointing; rush of happiness; to set apart for ministerial positions or for religious services.

English words that refer to anointing:

- Anoint - to anoint with oil.
- Anointed - a person set apart for God.

To arrive at a general description of anointing, let us combine the three languages.

Anointing - it is the act through which God sets someone apart. He develops their character, qualities and virtues, with the purpose of using them in His ministry.

"[10]But my horn shall Thou exalt like the horn of a unicorn; I shall be Anointed with fresh oil."
Psalms 92.10

"[6]And the Spirit of the LORD will come upon thee and thou shall prophesy with them and shall be turned into another man." 1 Samuel 10.6

The biblical definition for "anointing": anointing is when the Holy Spirit empowers, clothes, covers, and transforms the person's soul and spirit with His character, personality, qualities and virtues. The word "power" in Greek is "dunamis", which means the ability to obtain results. To define it in simple terms, we could say that **anointing is a "God Given Super-natural Power" to obtain exceptional results.**

Example: A singer might sing all right, but under the anointing he will be a sensational singer producing great results. Regardless of whether you are a minister, housewife, teacher, or other, when the anointing is upon you, the outcome of whatever you have set out to accomplish, will be unexpectedly good.

Examples and definitions of anointing

The anointing of the Holy Spirit is the endowment of supernatural abilities to sing, preach, teach, or do anything to serve Him and His Kingdom.

Examples of the anointing:

- When messages are spontaneous.

- When preaching creates changes in the lives of the listeners, even when proper grammar, homiletic or hermeneutic rules are overlooked.

- When the worship music ministers through the presence of God, regardless of whether the musicians are professional or not.

- When musicians or singers worship spontaneously, and the congregation is uplifted.

- When leaders minister to specific congregational needs.

   "[4]And my speech and my preaching were not with enticing words of man's wisdom, but in demonstration of the Spirit and of power, [5]that your faith should not stand on the wisdom of man, but on the power of God." 1 Corinthians 2.4, 5

- When people go to the altar brokenhearted, crying, or repenting of their sins, without using the power of persuasion.

- When someone unexpectedly ministers the Prophetic Word, as enlightened by the Holy Spirit, and directly speaks to the needs of the people.

How does the lack of anointing affect us?

Let us look at it in the following way. I have a microphone and I know how to use it. When it is turned on, I speak into it, and my voice is amplified. This is possible, not because of my ability to use the microphone or the sound equipment, but because of the electricity that flows through it. I know this because if the electricity is shut down, my effort to be heard will be in vain; my voice will not be amplified. In this same manner, without the anointing, our spiritual life is unfruitful. **The anointing is as vital to a minister as electricity is to the microphone.**

The anointing in the Old Testament

The anointing in the Old Testament only rested upon kings, priests and prophets. God separated these ministerial positions for the purpose of serving Him and His people. It is worth noting that the anointing was only temporary, it only rested upon an individual for a specific time and usually remained for only a short period of time.

The anointing in the New Testament

God gives us two types of anointing: the internal anointing and the special anointing or the anointing upon.

"20But ye have an unction from the Holy One, and ye know all things." 1 John 2.20

"13Jesus answered and said unto her: "Whosoever drinketh of this water shall thirst again, 14but whosoever drinketh of the water that I shall give him shall never thirst; but the water that I shall give him shall be in him a well of water springing up into everlasting life." John 4.13, 14

The Purpose of the internal anointing

- **To teach** - God uses the Internal anointing to teach us all things.

    "27But the anointing which ye have received from Him abided in you, and ye have no need that any man teach you. But as the same anointing teaches you of all things, and is truth and is no lie, and even as it hath taught you, ye shall abide in Him." 1 John 2.27

- **To guide** - The internal anointing provides inner testimony to our spirit; it guides us to all truth. -At one time, I found myself in a meeting where a woman was preaching. My heart kept telling me that her message was wrong.

Although I was a new believer, the internal anointing or the "anointing within" lead me to understand that her preaching was not of God. Later, some pastors published an article confirming that, indeed, she had been teaching false doctrine.

- **To develop Christ's character** - Christ's character is the "internal anointing or the anointing within us". This anointing enables us to bring forth fruit, love, kindness, gentleness and self-control. We cannot develop Christ's character without the internal anointing.

The "anointing upon" or "the special anointing"

"8But ye shall receive power after the Holy Spirit is come upon you; and ye shall be witnesses unto me both in Jerusalem, and in all Judea and in Samaria, and unto the uttermost part of the earth." *Acts 1.8*

The "anointing upon" helps us to fulfill God's calling and provides us with the ability to serve Him through the power of the Holy Spirit. The Word of God teaches that every Christian has received a certain level of the anointing. It guides and teaches all things. Some Christians receive a special anointing according to God's calling upon their lives.

When Jesus spoke of the anointing upon Him, He referred to it as "rivers of living water." Rivers provide water to many.

"[37]On the last day, that great day of the feast, Jesus stood and cried out, saying, 'If any man thirst, let him come unto me, and drink. [38]He that believeth in me, as the Scripture hath said, out of his belly shall flow rivers of living water.'" John 7.37, 38

The "special anointing" or the "anointing upon"

The special anointing:

- Prepares
- Sanctifies

The special anointing is given to fulfill God's calling. We can see this in the life of the Apostle Paul:

"[11]And God wrought special miracles by the hands of Paul, [12]so that handkerchiefs or aprons from his body were brought unto the sick, and the diseases departed from them and the evil spirits went out of them." Acts 19.11, 12

To better understand the anointing, let us summarize it in the following way: The anointing gives us the ability to obtain wonderful results in our ministry, our calling, business, family, and amongst ourselves. If we try to fulfill God's calling without the anointing, we will surely fail and the results will be far from positive.

The "internal anointing" allow us to develop Christ's character and to live as victorious Christians. This anointing enables us to give good testimonies and leave legacies of our lives. The "special anointing" was given to fulfill the calling of God in our lives.

We receive this anointing when we are born again and filled with the Holy Spirit; this becomes evident when we speak in other tongues.

We should constantly ask God to anoint us with this precious gift, which we desperately need in our lives.

The Anointing and Character

God expects us to have balanced lives. We should attempt to balance our character and charisma through the fruit of His Spirit and His power. Some leaders are placing too much emphasis on charisma and little importance on character. In this chapter, we will study charisma and character in more detail.

What is Charisma? Charisma is an exceptional ability to attract and influence others; it is a divinely inspired gift or power, which may include being used by the Holy Spirit to perform miracles and healing. Charisma is a freely given and unearned gift from God.

What is Character? Character is the inner moral nature, ethical strength, quality and ability; it is easily detected by the way we behave under pressure and it is demonstrated through our attitudes, actions, behavior and lifestyles. True character is reflected by the attitude one assumes when criticized, insulted or during a crisis, whether one is alone or in public. We reflect our character by our spontaneous reactions.

A leader's character is a fundamental part of his success in life and it is the foundation his ministry is built upon. The groundwork for his ministry is his charisma.

If the minister's character is strong and well founded, he will build strong ministries. If his character is weak, his ministry will be vulnerable to adverse circumstances and temptations.

Character weaknesses rapidly destroy what might take years to build. Poor character destroys our testimony and causes great conflict within the church, to the extent of breaking up marriages. These traits encompass a vast realm of consequences such as lies and sin; all are displeasing to God.

An example of this is a "Christian" musician and piano player living a double life. At home, he is a lousy dad and a bad husband, with an explosive personality. He is verbally abusive to his children and has no devotional life or intimacy with God. However, he does have a privileged voice and plays the piano very well. In this case, his ministry is based on specific talents, gifts and charisma, but not on his character. Eventually, his weak character will be his downfall.

How can someone with poor or weak character improve his or her life? His character must be transformed; this may be accomplished through Godly people who can help him develop his character. (These people might become his mentors; they will guide him, discipline him, love him, and help him mature.)

"[7] But unto every one of us is given grace according to the measure of the gift of Christ. [8] Therefore He said, "When He ascended up on high, He led captivity captive, and gave gifts unto men." [9] (Now the saying,

"He ascended" --what does it mean but that He also first descended into the lower parts of the earth? [10]He that descended is the same, who also ascended up far above all heavens, that He might fill all things.) [11]And He appointed some to be apostles, and some prophets, and some evangelists, and some pastors and teachers." Ephesians 4.7-11

Before appointing someone to a leadership position, we should always ask ourselves if that person's character reflects the character of Christ. We must consider if he lives with integrity, notice his character stability, and see if he is the same in private, as well as in public.

It is important that we know the difference between charisma and character. **Charisma** is a God given gift, a talent or ability; it cannot be earned or deserved. We are imparted with charisma when we are called into ministry. It is a gift received by grace, it does not take time to mature, and it allows us to carry out His purpose, effectively.

When called into the ministry, I received the gift of preaching; I am blessed with it.

Character is defined as a person's qualities and abilities. It is their inner nature and their moral or ethical strength; it is easily recognized by how someone reacts under pressure. Character is defined as the total sum of a person's positive and negative characteristics, as these reveal themselves in their daily walk. True character is manifested in adverse circumstances, which cause undue stress.

Let us take the example of a man in love. During the dating stage of the relationship, he was considerate, sweet, tender and courteous. After the wedding, when conflicts got the best of him, he began to experience pressures, started to complain, argue and curse. This was his true character; it manifested itself when life's pressures came upon him.

A person's character is revealed in six different areas:

Thoughts - Thoughts are a product of thinking, of concepts, opinions or judgments. Thoughts are what a person constantly meditates on, or thinks about. The Word tells us that:

"[7] For as he thinkest in his heart so is he."
Proverbs 23.7

Values - Values are defined as desirable qualities, important principles and standards that guide individual behavior. Values are beliefs that reveal the inner self.

Motivation - Motivation is the mental process or function that produces drive and incentive. It stems from character and may be considered the underlying behavior in life, causing reactions to specific situations. Proper or improper motivation determines personal nature, achievements, or lack of accomplishments.

Attitude - Attitude is the overall disposition indicative of state of mind and behavior. Positive or negative attitudes stem from personal character; they can be contagious. We must constantly examine our overall attitudes in life and observe our attitudinal changes.

Feelings - Feelings are emotional responses totally unrelated to reason and logic. Feelings are instant impressions produced by persons, places or situations. These can be repressed or expressed through personal character.

Actions - Action is the exterior physical process of conduct, behavior and movements. Action is energy in operation. Our actions should reflect our feelings, attitudes, motivations and values towards God and others.

We should constantly examine our thoughts, values, motivations, attitudes, feelings and actions, bringing them under submission, in Christ, in order to increase the anointing in our lives.

"[19]I can will what is right, but I cannot do it. For I do not do the good I want, but the evil I do not want is what I do." Romans 7.19

Charisma is a gift given by God; it does not have to be developed. It differs from character because character is progressive and not instantly acquired and developed through self-control, effort and submission.

In order to improve our character, we must deny our fleshly desires, crucify our flesh, die to ourselves and model Christ's character. **God expects us to improve in this area**.

Throughout my years in ministry I learned that God uses us more often as our character develops. Otherwise, the gifts and talents that we received might lead to our self-destruction. **Character is progressive and it is developed; charisma is instantly acquired, it does not increase.**

How is the character of Christ developed in us?

- **Through Gods' dealings with us** - God deals with us to develop our character. Sometimes in order to bring change into our lives, He confronts us, harshly.

- **Trials and tribulations** - Trials and tribulations mold, develop and improve our character.

There are personal qualities and character traits, which will increase the anointing in our lives.

In order to have a properly balanced ministry, leaders must posses certain virtues. Let us study some of them.

- **Integrity** - Integrity is a lifestyle of proper Christian values, standards and principles, which entail complete sincerity and honesty. It is also the state of being unimpaired, sound, complete, altogether, and being a moral person with good motivations. A person who does not reflect corruption, but instead is pure in spirit, soul and body, has integrity and is incorruptible.

- **Incorruptible** – A person who is pure of spirit, soul and body. When a person does not exhibit immoral behavior or impure motivations. A person who does not reflect corruption is said to be incorruptible.

"[7]In all things showing thyself to be a pattern of good works; in doctrine showing incorruptness, seriousness, sincerity." Titus 2.7

"[1]Rejoice in the LORD, O ye righteous! For praise is comely for the upright." Psalms 33.1

"[3]The integrity of the upright shall guide them, but the perverseness of transgressors shall destroy them." Proverbs 11.3

- **Humble** - To be humble is to recognize that everything that we have comes from God. It is to know who we are in Christ. We should be neither proud nor ashamed of who we are. To be humble is to give God the glory for our qualities. If we desire to minister in the anointing, we must walk in humility, always recognizing our total dependency upon God and giving Him all the glory. To be humble is also to consider all others greater than ourselves.

"[15]For thus said the high and lofty One who inhabited eternity, whose name is Holy: "I dwell in the high and holy place with him also that is of a contrite and humble spirit, to revive the spirit of the humble and to revive the heart of the contrite ones." Isaiah 57.15

- **Obedient - Godly** obedience is to do His Will, rather than ours. Obedience is a virtue that makes someone great before God's eyes. When God trusts someone with His anointing, He expects obedience. Jesus said, "I desire obedience, not sacrifice." **A small act of obedience can open great doors before God.** John the Baptist never healed the sick, raised anyone from the dead, parted the sea, nor performed any miracles; nevertheless, Jesus said this of him:

"[11]Verily I say unto you, among them that are born of women, there hath not risen a greater than John the Baptist; notwithstanding, he that is least in the Kingdom of Heaven is greater than he." Matthew 11.11

Question: What made John the Baptist great if he never performed any miracles? God considered John the Baptist great because he was obedient to

His calling. In other words, our obedience impresses the Lord and makes us great before His eyes. **Our obedience may not be that important to man, but it is vital to God.**

- **Submissive** - We are submissive when we allow someone whom is intellectually, morally and spiritually superior to us, to judge our actions or decisions. We must be accountable in all areas of our lives including our marriage, ministry, friendships, work and more. It is wise for every leader and every believer to be accountable to someone for their life. This is important for several reasons:

In order to have spiritual covering - We must be accountable to someone in leadership. When we make mistakes, we need correction. Our mentor must hold us accountable for our decisions, our family, our relationships, our ministry and the doctrine that we teach.

I believe there is not one man or woman who has climbed the spiritual ladder in ministry, who did not need a spiritual covering. Whether you are a prophet, apostle, teacher, evangelist, pastor, or reverend, you need a spiritual covering, although, this does not mean affiliation to any particular council.

As a Pastor, I am personally accountable to spiritually mature men. I do this voluntarily because of my values, based on a covenant relationship of love and fellowship. This does not adversely affect the ministry's vision in any manner.

There are many ministers, particularly performers, singers and musicians who serve the Lord, who do not hold their selves or their ministries accountable to anyone and this can be very dangerous. Everyone needs to be accountable to avoid falling into the pitfalls and temptations of life. Accountability is necessary to avoid false doctrine, sin or improper behavior.

To protect our life and ministry - In order for the ministry to grow, we must have spiritual covering. We must be accountable to someone willing to oversee our life and ministry. As pastors, we need to be ministered to, and we need to receive counseling.

However, we should never seek counsel within the congregation. Our mentors will confidently hear us, advice us and restore us when we need it. Our mentors must be above our level; Godly, wise and virtuous. We must submit to them in the same way in which we obey and submit to God; for our own benefit and protection.

To be pure - The word pure specifically refers to our motives and intentions. Through the Old Testament, we see that before someone received the anointing it was necessary for him to go through a period of cleansing. God would only pour His anointing upon clean and pure vessels.

Below are a few principles that you may want to apply to your life. I try to keep my motives and intentions pure by applying these principles.

A. Whatever you do for the kingdom, do it in the name of Jesus. When you do something in the name of Jesus, have the assurance He will back you up from the start.

"[17]And whatsoever ye do in word or deed, do all in the name of the Lord Jesus, giving thanks to God the Father by Him." Colossians 3.17

B. Whatever you do for the kingdom, do it with all your heart. Doing something with all your heart implies that you do it with all your might, strength and mind. Give it all you can give, and do it to please God and not to impress man. Whether you sing, preach or dance, whatever you do, always do it with all your heart.

"[23]And whatsoever ye do, do it heartily, as to the Lord and not unto men." Colossians 3.23

C. Whatever you do for the kingdom, do it for the Glory of God. You should not seek your own interest. Do not do anything half way or try to impress others. Your motivation should always be to bring honor and glory to the Kingdom of Christ.

To be compassionate - Compassion means to feel someone else's pain; to be deeply touched by a person's need. The more compassion we express towards the lost, the sick, or the one who is in sin, the greater the anointing will be upon our lives. Some believers have improper motives. They would like to have the healing anointing, yet they lack compassion for the sick. The true healing anointing does not flow without compassion. We see how Jesus felt compassion for the people in His miracles.

"[14] And Jesus went forth and saw a great multitude, and was moved with compassion toward them, and He healed their sick." Matthew 14.14

To be bold - Is to be fearless, daring and courageous. Boldness is a God given virtue, not a quality of human character. Boldness is the opposite of fear. This word comes from the Greek word *"parrhesia"*, meaning without hesitation, courageous, forward, audacious, daring and out- spoken.

In order to flow in the anointing, one must be bold. We must dare to be outspoken, speak boldly, and preach honestly and without fear on any subject. We should have the courage to cast out demons, and the strength to take great steps of faith that others may not dare to take. God will sometimes ask us to do certain things that may seem illogical or senseless to the human mind. Here is when we **must choose to activate or implement our God-given boldness.** Unless we take the initiative to implement boldness, we will never be used to the extent that God would like to use us with His anointing. Boldness is gradual and progressive. It is like a muscle; it needs to be exercised and developed. Like faith, boldness increases through its use, prayer and the Word.

When our church used to be at our previous location, I shared with the congregation that we were going to purchase the Temple where we are today. Many said that I was crazy, and that the building was too expensive. I continued to stand firm in the decision to buy it and to trust God. A year later, the temple was purchased at a price of three million dollars, even though we did not have that amount of money. Regardless of the negative comments, I trusted God to provide. His abundant provisions overflowed and we were able to buy the temple.

During the Miracle Crusades, God has asked me to do things for the sick that make no sense to me. By having **"activated boldness"** in my life, I have been obedient and we have seen innumerable healings and miracles. **I strongly believe that it is preferable to make a mistake as we try to obey God than to remain insensitively passive and disobey Him. We must discern wisely, and develop our sensitivity to the guiding of the Holy Spirit.**

Boldness is an important aspect of the believer's character. It enables us to move in the anointing, even though at times, we may not understand why we should do what we are asked to do, yet we do it because we know everything is going to be all right. Just obey the Holy Spirit; do not try to make sense of everything. Be daring and bold in the Spirit, speak the Word honestly, and **follow anything** that the Holy Spirit leads you to do.

To have unity - To have unity means to be of one mind, sharing only one purpose. It is the quality of harmony and agreement; the state of being combined into one. **There are certain conditions that open up the heavens and allow the anointing to be poured down: unity, prayer, tithes, and offerings.**

"[1] Behold, how good and how pleasant it is for brethren to dwell together in unity! [2] It is like the precious ointment upon the head that ran down upon the beard, even Aaron's beard that went down to the skirts of his garments." Psalms 133.1, 2

How can we apply this to our lives? Believers, who love unity, always have a greater anointing on their lives, regardless of whether they are in the body of Christ, in the local church, or in the family. The opposite of having a Spirit of Unity is to have a Spirit of Division. God considers division as an abomination; He loves all those who seek Him in unity. When there is unity, the anointing is more powerful.

To have Maturity - Maturity is the state or quality of being fully grown and developed. It consists in fully recognizing and rejoicing in who we are in Christ. It is being certain of our calling; it is not feeling threatened by someone else's accomplishments or success. Maturity means to be rooted in Christ, not in our ministry or church. We must be clear that the ministry and the church do not belong to us; they belong to God.

Many leaders and ministers are easily hurt and threatened by someone else's talents, abilities, and opinions, or by conflicting personalities. This is an immature attitude and somewhat common.

We are to be mature stewards of the anointing. The anointing is a precious Godly Gift that we must treasure. If we do not cherish our anointing, we may loose it.

Some of us are not "right before God", yet He may continue to use us, even though He may not approve of our present lifestyle. We may mistakenly think that He is pleased with us as we continue to live disruptive lives, not realizing that eventually, God's judgment will come.

We must develop certain important virtues, which should become part of our character, in order that our righteous walk may sustain the weight of the ministry. If our character develops to its full potential, then many aspects of our ministry are more likely to function properly.

CHAPTER 3

The Purpose of
the Anointing

What is the purpose of the anointing? What is the anointing used for? Unfortunately, many believers use it to glorify their ministry and for self-gratification.

Why will God anoint us? For what purpose does He anoint us?

1. God will anoint us so we can consecrate people, as well as things, for His service.

God will anoint, separate and consecrate persons, places or things for His service. The anointing enables us to do any thing for Him; regardless of how big, small or insignificant it may be. The anointing is the special manifestation of His Divine Power, given to us, so we may properly serve Him.

"[41]And thou shalt put them upon Aaron thy brother and his sons with him; and shall anoint them and consecrate them and sanctify them, that they may minister unto me in the priest's office."
Exodus 28.41

"[29]And the holy garments of Aaron shall be his sons' after him, to be anointed, Therein and to be consecrated in them." Exodus 29.29

2. The anointing enables us to fulfill our ministry.

His anointing separates, blesses and enables us to carry out powerful ministries through His strength. Without it, we become exhausted. Jesus said in Acts 1.8, **"But ye shall receive power after the Holy Spirit is come upon you."** Power means to have the strength and ability to do any God given job.

3. The anointing creates passion and zeal.

Passion and zeal are two things greatly needed in ministry, yet many ministers lack them. They do things on their own strength and eventually totally burn out, not only physically, but spiritually as well. We must learn to minister with God's passion and zeal.

"[17]And His disciples remembered that it was written: "The zeal of Thine house hath eaten me up." John 2.17

4. The anointing destroys the works of the devil.

The anointing breaks satanic yokes and oppressions. Since the enemy is unable to withstand God's Presence, there may be demonic manifestations in anointed services.

"[27]And it shall come to pass in that day, that his burden shall be taken away from off thy shoulder

and his yoke from off thy neck, and the yoke shall be destroyed because of the anointing." Isaiah 10.27

"[38]How God Anointed Jesus of Nazareth with the Holy Spirit and with power, and how He went about doing good and healing all who were oppressed by the devil, for God was with Him." Acts 10.38

"[8]He that committed sin is of the devil, for the devil sinneth from the beginning. For this purpose the Son of God was manifested, that He might destroy the works of the devil." 1 John 3.8

5. The anointing heals the broken hearted.

The Holy Spirit's anointing is medicine for the broken hearted and for those who are emotionally hurt. The church has often passed on our responsebility towards the mentally wounded by referring them to psychiatric and psychological treatment, rather than taking the time and interest to seek God and His anointing.

"[18]The Spirit of the Lord is upon me, because He hath anointed me to preach the Gospel to the poor. He hath sent me to heal the brokenhearted, to preach deliverance to the captives, and recovering of sight to the blind, to set at liberty them that are bruised." Luke 4.18

6. The anointing provides freedom.

The anointing brings deliverance from sins, addictions, bondages and oppressions. Some of us need deliverance from our previous emotional wounds, set ways of behavior and compulsive desires such as: sex, food, cursing and others. The anointing sets the captives free from oppression. Many people are constantly depressed, anxious and unable to sleep, while others continuously use prescription medicines to function during the day and sleeping pills to get through the night. They need deliverance from the yokes of addiction, oppression and depression. When we are in bondage, or oppressed, our primary objective should be, to be set free and healed that we may serve God more effectively.

7. The anointing is to glorify Jesus, not man.

Some ministers and entertainers have prostituted the anointing by seeking to glorify themselves instead of Jesus. The anointing should always glorify Jesus and His works. We must always determine who is to be exalted, Christ or self.

"13However, when He, the Spirit of Truth, is come, He will guide you into all truth; for He shall not speak from Himself, but whatsoever He shall hear, that shall He speak; and He will show you things to come. 14He shall glorify me, for He shall receive of mine, and shall show it unto you." John 16. 13, 14

8. The anointing empowers believers with God's gifts and ministries.

Every believer has a God given measure of grace in the anointing; therefore, we must act and minister upon it accordingly.

"[10]As every man hath received the gift, even so minister the same one to another as good stewards of the manifold grace of God." 1 Peter 4.10

The yokes of slavery hold people captive. The anointing of the Holy Spirit can destroy these yokes when it manifests itself through His church. Some strongholds are: the yokes of oppression, fear, sex, low self-esteem, sickness, addictions, drugs, alcoholism, etc.

When the presence of the anointing is powerful, demons cannot resist it. The Word of God teaches that the devil must flee from us when we resist him. It also says that the enemy came to kill, steal and destroy, and that Jesus appeared to destroy the works of the devil.

When the devil oppresses us through fears, we can call on Jesus to show up and deliver us from those oppressions. This is why He is the Anointed One. Glory to God!

"[10]The thief cometh not but to steal and to kill and to destroy. I am come that they might have life, and that they might have it more abundantly." John 10.10

Why do so many Christians live in defeat?

Many believers have not grasped the full significance of the concept that Jesus defeated the devil at the cross. We may not have fully understood that we are to live free of oppressions, without yokes or burdens. When we are in bondage by the Devil's schemes, we must learn to set ourselves free with the anointing of the Holy Spirit. This is the only way those bondages can be destroyed.

Once we are delivered, we must bless others and help set them free. **We have the anointing that Jesus had. The word "Christian" means "Anointed one", or called to set the captives free, to heal the broken hearted and to preach salvation.** When the anointing comes upon us, Jesus said that we might do greater works than He did. We are a powerful church and the gates of hell shall not prevail against us; nothing can stop us.

Let us remember that race, nationality, and intellectual levels are unimportant, because if the anointing is upon us, God will use us in mighty ways. The anointing can change a repressed and shy person into a bold and courageous believer. Jesus changed Peter, who cowardly denied Him three times. He transformed him into a new man, who powerfully preached the Word of God to a multitude, and 3,000 people received salvation.

The anointing may be imitated, and certain conditions may seem to be similar, but the outcome will be strange in nature. God's anointing is the result of fervent prayer. The anointing has distinctive qualities that separate true preaching of the Word from other methods used. The anointing penetrates and reinforces His truth with all of God's power.

The anointing enlightens and enriches the Word as it enables us to grasp and understand it. It prepares the heart of the preacher, and conditions it with tenderness, purity and light; which are essential conditions. These conditions are required for the heavenly anointing. The anointing is vital for every preacher, especially when ministering. The anointing may cause commotion in many congregations.

A sermon may be heard without any evidence of change, movement or agitation, and everything may be as still and as quiet as in a cemetery. Then you see another preacher under the mysterious anointing who gives the same sermon without deviating from the Word, and the Holy Spirit creates the anticipation of a powerful move of God. The change in the congregation is perceived, and something very special happens when the anointing comes upon the congregation! ... Amen, Glory to God!

The anointing penetrates and awakens the conscience, bringing conviction of sin. It also humbles the sinful heart, which lacks strength.

Preaching without the anointing will dry, harden, irritate and kill the message. It will be boring, and may cause sleep. Unanointed preaching (or without the anointing) will seek alternative ways of obtaining positive results, since it places emphasis on matters of less importance. We need Anointed men and women of God.

Christ is coming back soon. God is raising a generation of men and women who choose to deny themselves; who are courageous and totally committed to fearlessly and boldly preach the Word of God without compromising its principles. God is pouring out His Power upon these Godly Christians, who are begining to shake the world through the anointing of the Holy One.

The Lord demands our total surrender. Many of us have only given God certain areas of our lives, but we must keep in mind that He wants all of our life or nothing at all. Just as He gave us His all, He expects our total surrender, discipline and sacrifice.

CHAPTER 4

How can the Anointing be Activated?

Before we consider activating the anointing let us mention a couple of things. **God's Power is always present.** People often say: "I didn't feel the Presence of God in that meeting." Yet, God's Power was present with all of its attributes; whether it is at its highest or its lowest level. But unfortunately, it is not always activated. Let us look at the following example:

"[17]And it came to pass on a certain day, as He was teaching, that there were Pharisees and doctors of the law sitting by, who had come from every town of Galilee and Judea and Jerusalem. And the power of the Lord was present to heal them." Luke 5.17

As we can see in the Word, God's power is present to heal, to save the lost and to deliver them from bondages. God will manifest Himself in any way that He desires. When we continue to read this passage, we notice that only one person received healing, leaving the rest behind without their healing miracle. Why? Because lack of faith did not allow them to believe.

If the power and the anointing are always present, why are they not evident all the time? Why are so many people still in need of salvation? Why are so many still held captive by the enemy? The answer to these questions is because they have yet to learn how to receive the anointing.

How can the Holy Spirit's anointing be activated?

1. Through faith. Let us look at the Scriptures and see that we cannot activate the anointing without faith.

"[34] And when they had gone over, they came into the land of Gennesaret. [35] And when the men of that place learned of Him, they sent out into all that country round about, and brought unto Him all who were diseased. [36] And they besought Him that they might only touch the hem of His garment. And as many as touched were made perfectly whole."
Matthew 14.34-36

There is something very special about this scripture. It says: ***"when they learned of Him,"*** *We* know that faith comes by hearing the Word of God, as it is written in the following verse:

"[17] So then faith cometh by hearing and hearing by the Word of God." Romans 10.17

What happened? They heard of Him and faith entered their hearts, activating the power of God; enabling them to receive their healing. In this same way, when we believe God, the anointing is activated; we receive salvation, healing and deliverance. Glory to God!

Let us look at another example from the Word of God:

"[25]And a certain woman who had an issue of blood twelve years, [26]and had suffered many things under many physicians, and had spent all that she had and was no better, but rather grew worse, [27]when she had heard of Jesus, came up behind Him in the press of the crowd and touched His garment; [28]for she said, "If I may touch but His clothes, I shall be whole." [29]And straightway the fountain of her blood was dried up, and she felt in her body that she was healed of that plague. [30]And Jesus, immediately knowing in Himself that virtue had gone out of Him, turned about in the press of the crowd and said, "Who touched my clothes?" [31]And His disciples said unto Him, "Thou seest the multitude thronging thee, and sayest thou, `Who touched me?'" [32]And He looked round about to see her who had done this thing. [33]But the woman, fearing and trembling, knowing what had been done in her, came and fell down before Him and told Him all the truth. [34]And He said unto her, "Daughter, thy faith hath made thee whole. Go in peace, and be whole of thy plague." Mark 5.25-34

Once again, in these verses we can see how the Lord's anointing is activated through faith.

What did the woman do to receive her healing?

1. She heard of Jesus.

2. She acted on what she heard.

3. She "confessed". This word is quite interesting. In Greek, it means to "say it continuously". What did she say repeatedly? The Word of God, "If I may touch but His clothes, I shall be whole."

4. She received her miracle.

How is faith released? Confession releases our faith. It is the bridge between the spiritual world and the physical world. Faith activates God's power or God's anointing. Doubt stops the power of God from flowing through His people.

"22 And Jesus answering, said unto them, "Have faith in God." Mark 11.22

Faith is acting on God's word.

The woman with the issue of blood heard about Jesus and immediately acted on what she heard. Faith without anointing is faith without works, and it is dead. In order to activate the anointing in our life, we must have faith.

There are two determining factors in a miracle. One is the level of anointing on the person ministering and the other is the level of faith of the one receiving the miracle. As we can see in these two conditions, God has placed the responsibility on both people; on the one who is ministering the anointing and on the one who is receiving it. Team effort is required, since He has called us to serve as one body.

Persevering in the midst of faith is crucial. Some ministers have repeatedly laid hands on the same believers, without having any immediate results. However, because they persevered, they received the anointing and the miracles took place. This may have happened because they needed to receive or hear the Word for their faith to be increased. **In order to receive from God, faith is required.**

God's anointing is impregnated.

Throughout the Word of God, we see how the anointing was stored or impregnated in clothes, handkerchiefs and even in a prophet's bones.

"[21] And it came to pass, as they were burying a man, that, behold, they spied a band of men; and they cast the man into the sepulcher of Elisha. And when the man was let down and touched the bones of Elisha, he revived and stood up on his feet." 2 Kings 13.21

The healing anointing

We can learn a lot from the passage of the woman with the issue of blood with respect to the healing anointing. We can receive the healing anointing according to God's Will, but we cannot anoint ourselves. God blesses us with the anointing to preach, teach and to function in various ministerial positions.

This special power is not only a heavenly matter, but it is also a "tangible substance". Tangible means: capable of being recognized or felt by the sense of touch; or that it can be touched. We see how Jesus knew the exact moment that the anointing left Him. It was so tangible that He was aware that the power had left Him. The woman with the issue of blood was also aware of it. She expected to receive the power as it was transferred to her. Hence, healing power is transmitted from one person to another, especially through physical touch. An example of this is the laying on of hands.

"[19]And the whole multitude sought to touch him: for there went virtue out of him, and healed them all."
Luke 6.19

Another way to transfer God's power from one person to the other is by applying Anointed clothes or handkerchiefs upon anyone who needs healing or deliverance.

It is important to know that power can be stored or impregnated in clothes, as it was stored in Jesus' robe and in Peter's handkerchiefs or aprons.

"[12]...so that handkerchiefs or aprons from his body were brought unto the sick, and the diseases departed from them and the evil spirits went out of them."
Acts 19.12

God's power travels through our bodies just like electricity travels through the wires. Faith is the activating power of the anointing. A minister might have a great anointing, but if the person receiving it does not have the faith to receive from said minister, then the power is not transferred.

When ministering in a crusade in Costa Rica, a lady asked me to anoint her husband's pajamas. Her husband was hospitalized. He was hit by a passing train; it crushed him, destroying his entire stomach. It was impossible for doctors to operate; a chance for survival was non-existent. Then, I prayed for her. She went to the hospital and asked permission to put the pajamas on her husband. The next day, when she went to the hospital, her husband was sitting up in bed, eating. God had healed him and raised him up out of his deathbed. The anointing had been stored in the clothes and transferred.

Other things that will activate the Holy Spirit's anointing.

2. Through Music. The anointing will always be stronger when we adore God in the Spirit. Worship allows the anointing to descend with greater intensity, making the corporate anointing more powerful. **Praise brings the presence of God; worship produces miracles.**

"[25]And at midnight Paul and Silas prayed and sang praises unto God, and the prisoners heard them. [26]And suddenly there was a great earthquake, so that the foundations of the prison were shaken; and immediately all the doors were opened and everyone's bands were loosed." Acts 16. 25, 26

Praise and worship ministers should thoroughly know and understand the anointing before choosing the proper lyrics to sing prophetic worship. If a worship song is sung at the wrong time, it can completely ruin a service. Worship leaders must be sensitive and 'pleasingly obedient' to the Holy Spirit.

3. Through Unity. Some leaders might minister under a strong personal anointing, but the corporal anointing is even stronger, and it descends upon ministers when the entire body of Christ is in one accord, in one mind and one purpose. God loves unity, as a result, He sends a greater anointing upon those who worship and seek Him as one.

[m1] Behold, how good and how pleasant it is for brethren to dwell together in unity! [2]It is like the precious ointment upon the head that ran down upon the beard, even Aaron's beard that went down to the skirts of his garments. It is as the dew of Harmon, [3]and as the dew that descended upon the mountains of -Zion; for there the LORD commanded the blessing, even life for nevermore." Psalms 133.1-3

When we come together, we must seek unity. To be united means to have one mind and one purpose, especially as we praise and worship God. God's power is always present, but not always activated or received. It is up to the person receiving the anointing to activate the power through his faith. In addition, in order to activate God's anointing, the temple needs to be saturated with powerful praise and worship.

Musicians must consecrate and separate themselves for God, not only in the technical side of it, but in the spiritual aspect as well.

I strongly believe that musicians must be musically, spiritually and technically prepared. When we meet to worship God, we should all be of one accord, one mind, and one purpose. This produces unity and the result is the presence of the corporal anointing, which ministers as it touches the Body of Christ.

Let us review some points. The anointing is stored in clothing. It is biblically correct to pray over handkerchiefs or clothes, not because the clothing has power, but they serve as a point of contact. We should never use handkerchiefs as amulets; what we have to do is anoint the garments. The anointing heals and sets the captives free, producing miracles.

People often ask me to anoint and pray over handkerchiefs. Once these are placed on the sick people, they received their healing. This is biblical, just as Jesus and Paul did it, we can do it too.

CHAPTER 5

The Anointing in the Five Ministries

Every believer receives the anointing to develop the gifts. Each of the five ministries receives a different anointing to fulfill the calling of God. This is a greater anointing than the one given to the other gifts and ministries.

"28And God hath set some in the church: first apostles, secondarily prophets, thirdly teachers, after that miracle workers, then those with gifts of healing, helpers, administrators, and those with diversity of tongues."
1 Corinthians 12.28

God gave the church five ecclesiastic offices and ministries.

- Apostles
- Prophets
- Pastors
- Evangelists
- Teachers

God has also given the church other ministries; let us take a closer look:

"6Having then gifts differing according to the grace that is given to us: if prophecy, let us prophesy according to our portion of faith; 7or ministry, let us wait on

our ministering; or he that teaches, on teaching; [8]or he that exhorted, on exhortation; he that giveth, let him do it with simplicity; he that ruleth, with diligence; he that showed mercy, with cheerfulness." Romans 12.6-8

These ministries have a certain level of anointing. However, when we speak of the five main ministries the anointing is different; it is greater and it is given at a higher level. You may serve in any of these ministries, but you need to find out exactly what your calling is to be able to serve effectively.

Each one of us receives the anointing to serve in certain areas. If we operate outside this scope, the anointing will not back us up and we will be unable to truly bless the Body of Christ.

THE APOSTOLIC ANOINTING

What is an apostle? The word apostle in Greek means one who is sent, a special messenger, a delegate and a commissioner with specific assignments. Many ministers call themselves apostles, when in reality they are not.

We will study some biblical characteristics of true apostles.

Characteristics of an apostle:

"[28]And God hath set some in the church: first apostles, secondarily prophets, thirdly teachers, after that miracle workers, then those with gifts of healing, helpers,

70

administrators, and those with diversity of tongues."
1 Corinthians 12.28

Apostles are first in rank. The apostolic ministry has greater power, authority and anointing than any other ministry. Some other ministries are: Prophet, Evangelist, Pastor and Teacher. Apostles have a higher rank; they will receive their anointing and authority accordingly. Just as all the ministries have different ranks, the angels and demons also have ranks.

Every believer has received authority as well as anointing. The five ministries have superior authority and anointing, but the strongest power is that of the apostles.

Apostles are pioneers. A pioneer is one who is first to establish himself in a territory. It is one who God has appointed and anointed to open and prepare the way for others to follow into new areas. Apostles receive the anointing to preach new truths, establish new believers and invade new territories.

Apostles have the ability to plant churches. An unmistakable sign of an apostle is the God given ability to establish new churches. Unfortunately, some pastors have never established a new church and improperly call themselves apostles.

"[6]I have planted, Apollo's watered, but God gave the increase." 1 Corinthians 3.6

Apostles have an anointing to breakthrough or to destroy. Breakthrough defines the act or ability to penetrate beyond an obstacle, to invade beyond the enemy's line of defense.

"[27] And it shall come to pass in that day, that his burden shall be taken away from off thy shoulder, and his yoke from off thy neck, and the yoke shall be destroyed because of the anointing." Isaiah 10.27

An apostle's teaching and preaching provides breakthrough or deliverance of strongholds. Some strongholds are: pride, finances, traditions, addictions, religiosity and set ways of thinking. All these strongholds may be broken through the apostolic breakthrough anointing.

Apostles have the ability to convey Godly Gifts. Apostles will impart Godly Gifts and Grace to prepare believers to do God's will.

"[11] For I long to see you, that I may impart unto you some spiritual gift, to the end ye may be established..." Romans 1.11

Apostles identify and train church leaders.

"[21] And when they had preached the gospel to that city, and had taught many, they returned again to Lystra, and to Iconium, and Antioch, [22] confirming the souls of the disciples, and exhorting them to continue in the faith, and that we must through much tribulation enter into the kingdom of God. [23] And when they had ordained them elders in every church, and had prayed with fasting, they commended them to the Lord, on whom they believed." Acts 14.21-23

Apostles minister in signs and wonders. Signs and wonders must accompany the ministry of an apostle.

"[3]And I was with you in weakness, and in fear, and in much trembling. [4]And my speech and my preaching was not with enticing words of man's wisdom, but in demonstration of the Spirit and of power: [5]That your faith should not stand in the wisdom of men, but in the power of God." 1 Corinthians 2.3-5

Apostles are highly persecuted. Apostles are persecuted when they preach the Word or for being pioneers in different areas. One of the most powerful teachings in the ministry of the apostle is deliverance.

THE PROPHETIC ANOINTING

What is a prophet?

A prophet is one who speaks in the name of God. He can speak about the past, present or future. The Bible refers to Old Testament prophets as a "seers", since they had Godly visions and revelations. Prophets receive enlightenment by instant revelations and are suddenly inspired to speak.

What are the characteristics of a prophet?

A prophet moves with power in the gifts of revelation. These gifts are: word of knowledge, word of wisdom, and the discernment of spirits.

Prophets have the ability to see the spirit world. Prophets receive these gifts to see future dangers that others may overlook, as well as supernatural visions.

Prophets must always operate in other ministries. Sometimes prophets are pastors, evangelists and teachers, but they must flow in the prophetic. There are certain combinations of the prophetic ministry such as: Prophet-Evangelist, Prophet-Pastor, Prophet-Teacher, and Prophet-Teacher-Pastor-Evangelist.

There is a distinctive difference between being a Prophet and prophesizing. Believers can prophesize, yet this does not make them Prophets. However, all Prophets must prophesize. - **The objective of the New Testament Prophecy is to edify the body of God, to console and to encourage believers.**

Prophets bring prophetic visions. Prophets receive revelations, through dreams and visions according to the Word of God. Prophets are seers, who see God's plans and purposes before they manifest.

"[7]Surely the Lord GOD will do nothing, but he revealed his secret unto his servants the prophets."
Amos 3.7

"[10]See, I have this day set thee over the nations and over the kingdoms, to root out, and to pull down, and to destroy, and to throw down, to build, and to plant."
Jeremiah 1.10

Prophets have great authority. Their prophetic authority enables them to uproot, pullout and destroy, all diabolic strongholds. Prophets can also edify and multiply the kingdom of God.

"[10]So I prophesied as he commanded me, and the breath came into them, and they lived, and stood up upon their feet, an exceeding great army."
Ezekiel 37.10

Prophets activate the gifts of the Spirit. The Prophetic anointing brings within itself the ability to activate the gifts of the Spirit. Their messages impart gifts and ministries to believers. Prophets will awaken believers who are not well rooted, and they will establish those that are lost or cold.

"[32]And Judas and Silas, being prophets also themselves, exhorted the brethren with many words, and confirmed them." Acts 15.32

Prophets will confirm the issues of God. God has created the ministry of the prophet to: confirm, strengthen, establish, remove doubts and bring new affirmations. When prophets confirm God's calling, visions, words or decisions, the body is continually strengthened and growing in the Lord.

Prophets are helpers in the house of the Lord.

"[1]Then the prophets, Haggai the prophet, and Zechariah the son of Iddo, prophesied unto the Jews that were in Judah and Jerusalem in the name of the God of Israel, even unto them. [2]Then rose up Zerubbabel the son of Shealtiel, and Jeshua the son of

Jozadak, and began to build the house of God which is at Jerusalem; and with them were the prophets of God helping them." Ezra 5.1, 2

Whenever there is a mighty move of God in a geographic area, satanic opposition arises. The Lord sends prophets to help local Pastors to combat the enemy's attack. **Prophets serve as spiritual radars that quickly identify any of the devils' strategies.**

PASTORS' ANOINTING

Who is a Pastor? A Pastor is one who has been Anointed to feed, watch, guide and care for the flock.

What are the responsibilities of a Pastor?

To feed. The congregation must receive the Word of God. Every Pastor has been given the ability to teach since this a way to care for the sheep.

To guide. A Pastor directs and guides the people to follow God's Will for that congregation through example and inspiration. One of the most important issues a Pastor must know is God's vision for that city, so he may properly guide them to accomplish the goal.

To watch. A pastor has the responsibility to keep his sheep from false doctrines, to correct those who rebel and to restore those who have fallen.

To care. The pastor must care for his sheep in all realms: spiritually, emotionally and physically. He must be like the good father who is always there for his children.

A pastor has many functions, but his most crucial priority before God is to pray and study the Word so he may properly feed his flock.

A pastor cannot adequately function unless he has the specific anointing to serve as a pastor; without this anointing, the church will not grow. The minister, who lacks the anointing needed to be a Pastor, will not have the energy to properly carry out all the duties that a pastor must fulfill.

What are the characteristics of a pastor?

A pastor has a loving heart and he loves being with people. He intercedes and cares for his city, and looks for the lost sheep. The pastor must be husband to only one wife. His married life should be an example to the congregation, and his wife and children must be submissive to him. I Timothy 3:1-7.

The pastor is patient with his sheep and loves them just as they are; he waits patiently for them to change.

THE EVANGELIST'S ANOINTING

Evangelist means one who brings good news. Notice that they are "good news", not condemnation nor judgment. The message that an evangelist bears must bring reconciliation between God and man.

"[5]Then Philip went down to the city of Samaria, and preached Christ unto them. [6]And the people with one accord gave heed unto those things, which Philip spoke, hearing and seeing the miracles, which he did. [7]For unclean spirits, crying with a loud voice, came out of many who were possessed with them; and many taken with palsies and who were lame, were healed."
Acts 8.5-7

What are the characteristics of an evangelist?

An evangelist receives the anointing to do signs and wonders. God equips evangelists with the gifts of healing and miracles. They direct the evangelic messages directly to the unbelievers who often need to see the power of God demonstrated in action through healings and miracles.

An evangelist's anointing is specifically for unbelievers. God has anointed his message to touch non-believers; the message is Jesus Christ crucified. God has enabled him to proclaim reconciliation and to encourage others to seek God's forgiveness through Jesus at the cross of Calvary.

An evangelist has a passion for souls. God has strongly anointed him with great passion to minister TO those who do not know Jesus; he loves the lost and souls are his burden.

An evangelist travels constantly. His main ministry is outside the church. He goes out, throws the net and brings the fish into the local church.

An evangelist must have pastoral covering. God has equipped evangelists within a body; they are not to work alone. No one is independent; everyone should be accountable to someone else.

THE TEACHER'S ANOINTING

The anointing of a teacher is one to instruct and teach biblical truths to many. God imparts teachers with an anointing to edify the body of the church and to lead it to maturity.

The difference between the evangelist and the teacher is that the evangelist proclaims to the non-believer. The evangelist speaks daringly and forcefully; he will exhort, edify and encourage the non-believer. **The anointing of a teacher will edify the church through the instruction of biblical truths.**

What are the characteristics of a teacher?

The teacher has great love and passion for seeking the scriptures. The teacher loves to study, search, and look into the Word. They want to know the root of all biblical truths; they seek references in dictionaries and commentaries; and before they teach, they seek God and pray.

The teacher has passion for the city's growth, while the evangelist loves the lost. The teacher strives to see the body of Christ grow through His Word. They want them to know the Word and to live by it.

The teacher constantly travels while ministering to the Body of Christ. The evangelist also travels often.

The anointing of teachers leads them to edify the Body of Christ. God has gifted teachers to instruct the Body of God, to teach biblical principles and to demonstrate how these can be applied to daily life.

Ministering in the wrong ministry

In the Old Testament, if someone was in the wrong ministry and entered into the Holy of Holies, he would instantly die. When someone is in a ministry without the anointing, then he is outside the will of God and that ministry will not grow. The presence of God will not be evident in them and they may even die prematurely.

It is imperative that each member of the Body of Christ identifies the ministry for which he/she has been specifically anointed for, whether it is as an apostle, prophet, teacher, evangelist or pastor. We must pray and ask God to reveal to us the specific ministries where we should serve Him.

When we are in the proper ministry, the anointing will back us up, the ministry will grow, people will be touched, lives transformed, and the name of Jesus exalted.

There is a well-known man of God in the United States to whom Jesus appeared in a vision, while he was in his room, and He spoke to him for almost three hours.

During this time, Jesus told him that many ministers had died at an early age, between 40 and 50, because they were in the wrong ministry.

Be sure that you are operating within God's calling and in the proper ministry, so that the anointing will back you up.

Remember, that the anointing of God is within His purpose for your life.

CHAPTER 6

The Price of
the Anointing

A nyone who desires to grow in a greater anointing should be careful not to be enticed by the glory, the preeminence or the benefits of the anointing; Most people only see the results of the anointing, the miracles, the power, signs and wonders that go on the altar. We may never realize the high price we need to pay to be used by God, or the personal sacrifices He requires.

Once, while studying about the anointing and getting ready to write on how to develop it, God asked me *"Are you willing to pay the price?"* I answered *"What price?"* and He answered *"The price of loneliness, peer pressures, difficult circumstance; the pressures of physical and mental fatigue; the price of self-denial; the price of seeking My face and My Word while others have fun or sleep."*

Truly Anointed leaders always have to pay a high price. The more effective the leader, the higher the price he has to pay. If you are willing to accept the challenge of being an Anointed leader who will influence your generation, you must be ready to pay the high price through the responsibility that this requires. Anointed leaders must endure many trials, challenges, and difficulties; but in this chapter we will study the most common. In the book of Matthew, Jesus explains this in detail:

"25But Jesus called them unto Him and said, "Ye know that the princes of the Gentiles exercise dominion over them, and they that are great exercise authority upon them. 26But it shall not be so among you; but whosoever will be great among you, let him be your minister; 27and whosoever will be chief among you, let him be your servant, 28even as the Son of Man came not to be ministered unto, but to minister, and to give His life as a ransom for many." Matthew 20.25-28

We will study the most common challenges in this chapter.

The word *"grand or great"* in Greek means large; one who wants to be in front of. An Anointed leader is one who wants to lead others. Jesus continues to say *"he will be your servant."* The word servant is *"diakono"* which means: a servant who is willing to supply others' needs. Then Jesus continues by saying, *"whoever wants to be first"* and what He means is, whoever wants to be a leader with authority should be a servant first. The word servant is *"doulos"*, which means a constant slave of others.

What lesson does Jesus show His disciples? He says that whoever wants to be a leader must have a special anointing and must first be a servant to all. The anointing is not for self-gratification, but to supply the needs of the Body of Christ. God will not give a special anointing to someone who lacks a servant's heart, who is uninterested in the Body of Christ or who is not willing to pay the high price for the anointing.

What price must Anointed leaders pay to be used by God?

1. Death of ego- Surrender, sacrifice and self-denial.
2. Rejection
3. Criticism
4. Loneliness
5. The pressure of making proper decisions
6 Fatigue

We will discuss each of the above terms in more detail in the following pages.

1. Death of ego.

Being a leader demands the commitment to serve others and to put other's needs above their own. Leaders who are concerned about their own goals, desires and objectives are not true Anointed leaders. Godly leaders must be willing to sacrifice their own personal desires and objectives to help others.

"[17]From henceforth let no man trouble me, for I bear in my body the marks of the Lord Jesus."
Galatians 6.17

"[39]He that findeth his life, shall lose it; and he that loseth his life for My sake, shall find it."
Matthew 10.39

Those born to be leaders within God's purpose cannot avoid paying the high price of personal sacrifice. Keep in mind that true Anointed leaders have discovered their own purpose and objectives as well as the vision which is worth dying for. **You will never be able to change your generation unless you are willing to die for that change. True greatness in life is in the willingness to die for the proper cause.**

Paul the Apostle speaks of the personal sacrifice he had to pay.

"[4] ... but in all things commending ourselves as the ministers of God in much patience: in afflictions, in necessities, in distresses, [5] in stripes, in imprisonment's, in tumults, in labors, in sleeplessness, in fasting; by [6] pureness, by knowledge, by long-suffering, by kindness, by the Holy Spirit, by love unfeigned."
2 Corinthians 6.4-6

2. Rejection

One of the consequences of being an Anointed leader is that you will be rejected. If you are willing to accept the high calling for your generation, then **prepare yourself** for rejection, and to be misunderstood by others. Everyone who wants to be accepted, and to belong as an Anointed leader, must pay the consequences, including being rejected because you live in holiness and integrity. Your living testimony of being an Anointed leader will bring conviction of sin to those around you. As a result, resistance and opposition may develop just as Jesus experienced it.

True Anointed leaders bring change; and change in its nature, produces conflict and resistance.

Why are leaders rejected?

Leaders challenge others to change their lifestyles, for this reason they are rejected. Most people refuse to listen when told they must change because they do not want to change.

Godly leaders should preach that God is a Holy God and that we must live in holiness. They should point out sin and its consequential effects. They should not compromise controversial issues such as: abortion, homosexuality, bigotry, hatred, etc. Others will dislike what we tell them when we exhort them to come out of their mediocrity and to live in holiness and victory.

Leaders are the "tabanos" of God.

Leaders are God's "Tabanos" or horseflies. This insect bites people while they sleep. During the time the Spaniards came to America, the Indians fought against them. The Indian chief, to protect the village, would leave one of his children keeping watch at night, who at times would fall asleep and stop watching. To prevent them from falling asleep while on duty, he would place a horsefly inside the watchtower. This solved the problem of keeping his son from falling asleep, ensuring that he would remain alert and on guard. Anointed leaders are society's horseflies, especially for believers without vision, or those that serve out of convenience and not commitment; they are casual believers, without purpose. They are carnal, spiritually warm, and lack conviction. God's horseflies encourage the people to change from mediocrity to excellence, in Christ.

Rejection doesn't mean you were mistaken, but it does indicate that you are daring others to change. Remember what the Word says:

"[10]Blessed are those who have been persecuted for the sake of righteousness, for theirs is the kingdom of heaven." Matthew 5.10

A man is totally accepted when he is totally rejected. Rejection is part of God's plan for our success, it's unavoidable. All anointed leaders who have influenced a nation, have been misunderstood and rejected.

3. Criticism

Every leader must identify with this reality. In other words, criticism is a part of our lifestyle and we must learn to live with it; we cannot escape it. The greatest test of a leader's maturity, conviction and commitment to the vision, is demonstrated in the attitude we have when faced with criticism. Our humility will never undergo more crucial tests than at these intense times. When we are ready to be criticized, then we are ready to be leaders.

The role of effective leaders will determine the direction of many lives. It entails taking specific positions about issues, as well as making crucial decisions. This always requires having to confront negative reactions, but true leaders never allow criticism to affect them.

Criticism is an opportunity to test our commitment and conviction. If we do not want criticism, then the only choice left is to do nothing.

It is preferable to receive criticism for doing something, than to be ignored for not doing anything at all.

"[11]Blessed are ye when men shall revile you and persecute you, and shall say all manner of evil against you falsely for My sake. [12]Rejoice and be exceeding glad, for great is your reward in Heaven; for so persecuted they the prophets who were before you." *Matthew 5.11, 12*

4. Loneliness

As leaders, we must be ready to stand-alone and to always be in front of our followers. The closer we get to God, the lonelier we may feel, but it is then that God himself sanctifies and transforms us, as His presence changes us. When we apply these concepts to our lives, people will think we are strange; often we will be misunderstood and sometimes regarded as crazy.

Why is this? Because others are not at our level of prayer, revelation or holiness; therefore, as leaders we may feel lonely many times, but keep in mind that the loneliest people are the ones who are entrusted with a message, a dream or a vision. Leaders who changed and influenced their generations were all lonely souls, and those who depend on other's approval, will encounter difficulties. The path of leadership is to walk alone; this is part of the price of being a good leader. I can love people and share with them, yet they are not my only source of fulfillment.

Jesus is the source of fulfillment. He is the true example of a leader. All of His disciples abandoned Him in His most crucial moment, yet He stood by His commitment and carried out His purpose. **Unless you are willing to stand-alone for your vision, others will not be willing to stand by you.**

5. The pressure of making proper decisions

Leaders will inevitably face many challenges, demands and responsibilities that are fundamental in leadership. They will be required to make critical decisions under internal and external pressures. Before making crucial decisions, Anointed leaders should previously consider all issues, information and opinions. Always seek God's will and wisdom. Before making any decisions, we must implement these steps. The stress produced by these burdens affect the emotional, physical and mental being, and if these are handled in an improper manner, they can become overly stressful.

Very few 'followers' are aware of all the demands that operate in leaders' lives. Most are unaware of the pressures and criticism leaders have to live with. Now there is a question that arises from all this, are we pleasing God or man?

"¹⁰For do I now persuade men, or God? Or do I seek to please men? For if I yet sought to please men, I should not be the servant of Christ." Galatians 1. 10

6. Fatigue

There are very strong demands on leadership, particularly in the mental and the physical areas. It is impossible to become a great leader without being affected by physical and emotional stress.

At times, upon returning from a Healing and Miracles Crusade, God has asked me to pray, and even though I was exhausted and felt that I did not have any physical strength left to pray, I did it because... if He asks us to pray, we must do it.

Prayer is necessary - God requires it.

If you are willing to work harder, longer, more intensely and way beyond your scope of responsibilities, you will be an effective leader. For this reason, leaders must incorporate a healthy diet and lifestyle to be physically fit. **When someone is physically and mentally exhausted, he will be more vulnerable to the enemy's temptations. The devil will wait until we are at our weakest moment to attack.**

Suggestions to be taken into consideration when experiencing fatigue:

* Do not make any important decisions; your mind is not clear to properly reason.

- Do not stay alone anywhere; the enemy may be setting a trap.
- Seek Gods' Presence; His Presence is the best place to receive strength.

The high cost of leadership. If we are willing to pay the cost of the anointing, then we are ready to be leaders. We should not expect to live normal lives, like others.

All of our time, talents and experiences are to be used for the service of others. We will undoubtedly influence the lives of our family and friends to the point that they too, will have to pay the price along with us. As leaders, we must be careful to balance our time between serving others, and the responsibility and obligations of family life.

We have studied about the anointing, what it is, and what it is not. Also, we have learned its purpose and how to activate it, how it relates to the five ministries and the price we must pay for the anointing. In the following chapter, we will look at this heavenly substance and learn how to minister it.

CHAPTER 7

How to Minister the Anointing

L et us now study how to minister under the beautiful power that rests upon us and how we can transfer it.

1. **By the laying on of hands.** This is one way that Jesus ministered the anointing. It saturates our whole being comprised of spirit, soul and body, which is transferable through the 'law of contact and transfer.' In other words, the anointing is transferable. When this law is in effect, certain positive or negative conditions may be transferable or transmitted from one person to another.

Example:

- **Jesus**

  "[40]Now when the sun was setting, all those who had any sick with divers diseases brought them unto Him; and He laid His hands on every one of them, and healed them." Luke 4.40

- **Peter and John**

  "[1]Now Peter and John went up together into the temple at the hour of prayer, being the ninth

hour. ²And a certain man lame from his mother's womb was being carried, whom they laid daily at the gate of the temple, ³which is called Beautiful, to ask alms from those who entered into the temple. ⁴He, seeing Peter and John about to go into the temple, asked for alms. And Peter, fastening his eyes upon him with John, said, "Look on us." ⁵And he gave heed unto them, expecting to receive something from them. ⁶Then Peter said, "Silver and gold have I none, but such as I have, I give thee: in the name of Jesus Christ of Nazareth, rise up and walk." Acts 3.1-6

Why the laying on of hands?

We are to use our hands as instruments to transmit God's anointing to others; and to fulfill the commandment that Jesus gave us to go out and minister healing to the world. The laying on of hands accomplishes many things:

- ❑ Impart healing
- ❑ Set the captives free from bondage
- ❑ Transfer the infilling of the Holy Spirit
- ❑ Restore believers' lives

At times, when God's anointing rested on me, I felt heat and electricity go through my hands.

2. **Through the spoken word.** Jesus ministered the anointing through the laying on of hands and on occasion, He simply spoke the Word.

"[8]The centurion answered and said, "Lord, I am not worthy that You should come under my roof. But only speak a word, and my servant will be healed." Matthew 8.8

The Holy Spirit must guide every believer, so that he will know and understand the methods God wants him to use, when ministering to the people.

The anointing and the Word. The way God uses to back himself up is through His Word. If we want the anointing to back us up wherever we go, we need to preach and speak the Word. Some may ask, "Why isn't there anything happening in our ministry?" The answer to this question may be as simple as, check the Word being preached. The anointing in our lives will confirm the spoken Word.

3. **Through the gifts of the Holy Spirit.** God has given us nine gifts of the Holy Spirit to equip His saints and to fulfill our individual ministries. Sometimes the anointing flows through these gifts.

We should never set limits on God, raise barriers or place conditions for God's anointing. It is important to understand that God uses more than the three ways previously mentioned to flow in the anointing because He does it according to His Will.

The Holy Spirit's anointing blesses the minister. It is not for self-gratification or for our own

99

benefit. When I need healing, I have to receive it by faith, just like every other believer. Even though I am a minister of the Word under the healing anointing, I could not use my anointing to receive my own healing; I had to implement faith.

ANOINTING QUENCHERS

If circumstances have saddened or grieved the Holy Spirit, the anointing will not appear. Every minister should create an atmosphere where the anointing can flow.

Lack of reverence. This is one of the mayor reasons why the anointing of the Holy Spirit does not manifest in some ministries. There are churches allowing kids to run around in the halls during the worship service. Also, people talk or are mere spectators of what is going on around them, and some even make fun of what happens during the time the anointing is present.

The first step to minister in the anointing is to be reverent. If we love God's anointing, distractions cannot be allowed and order must be strictly enforced. Our goal should always be to please God and not men. In order to honor God's anointing, we MUST demand reverence, even at the cost of being arrogant and bossy.

Fear of breaking men's traditions. When the Holy Spirit descends with His anointing, our fear of going against established traditions may become an impediment.

At times, it is easier to follow tradition than to seek God's anointing. Unfortunately, when a new move of the Holy Spirit is evident, people may choose to close themselves off to it, making it very difficult for God to move in their midst.

"6 ... then he need not honor his father or mother. Thus you have made the commandment of God of no effect by your tradition." Matthew 15.6

Lack of desire for the anointing. Lack of hunger for the anointing grieves the Holy Spirit; therefore, it is imperative that a great desire for the manifestation of God's anointing to saturate the services be present. In our church, this is a common occurrence.

Abundance of sin. In order for the Spirit of God to manifest Himself freely and to flow in the anointing, we must be clean godly vessels.

In conclusion, we can say that when we learn to flow in the Holy Spirit's anointing, any of these methods previously mentioned will be effective. All detrimental conditions destroying the anointing, and often found in churches, must be eliminated. We must have great zeal, reverence and desire, for the Holy Spirit to flow in our lives and in our church.

Developing the Anointing

If there were any formulas to develop the anointing, they would have been already developed. We will study certain experiences that have proven to increase the anointing in great men of God, as well as in ourselves.

The level of anointing in someone's life is dependent upon several factors: God's calling, dedication, consecration, and surrender.

God's calling. God calls everyone, but some may have a special calling. The Lord may have blessed some with a special anointing because they are specifically valuable for His purpose.

Dedication and consecration. We must consecrate and dedicate ourselves totally to Him.

Surrender. We must live in full surrender of our lives to His service and will.

The level of anointing developed in us is relative to our surrender, compromise and consecration to God. There are people who have neither consecrated nor dedicated their lives to the Lord. In other words, to have the call of God is not sufficiently enough to truly flow in the anointing.

How can we increase the anointing in our lives?

1. By influences

The influence of Anointed men and women of God is a pre-requisite to accelerate the increase of the anointing in our lives. Pastors, ministers and leaders must be Anointed, Godly people, because they provide us with our spiritual covering and affect our lives, daily. Anointed leaders will positively affect our lives, but if the leader is not anointed, he can affect us in negative ways.

2. Our environment

Our environment should be full of God's anointing, as it will affect our lives positively or negatively. We should carefully choose our environment, so that it may properly influence us.

3. Our relationships

Believers who desire to increase the anointing in their lives should associate themselves with spirit-filled ministries, churches, pastors and leaders. Close friends should also be anointed.

"¹Behold, how good and how pleasant it is for brethren to dwell together in unity! It is like the precious ointment upon the head that ran down upon

the beard, even Aaron's beard that went down to the skirts of his garments." Psalms 133.1, 2

The anointing flows from above to beneath. Each one of us should understand the following biblical principle: **"The anointing, which is above the head, will flow throughout the whole body."** If our spiritual covering or leader is cold and dry, their same condition flows downward to us. How does this happen? Through influence, the environment and by association, anything can be passed down.

Many of our leader's personal characteristics are passed on to us. When we are under someone's covering, we receive his or her same conditions. Some of these may be: fear, doubt, sin, apathy, or unbelief. Instead of becoming anointed leaders, we may become miserably defeated believers. When we are under Anointed leadership, their positive traits are transferred to us. Some of these traits are: faith, strength, obedience, humility, discipline, wisdom, etc.

In order to maximize the anointing in our lives we should:

❑ Associate with Anointed Godly people.

❑ Remain within Anointed environments.

❑ Be influenced by Anointed men and women of God.

❑ Develop a lifestyle of fasting and prayer.

To increase the anointing in our lives we must be in Anointed environments and in ministries equipped with Godly people. For example: Elijah and Elisha, Moses and Joshua, Jesus and His disciples. We must spend time with Godly men and women, who continually walk with Christ.

4. By developing lifestyles of fasting and prayer

Throughout scripture, we see that all Anointed people had powerful prayer lives. They sacrificed their family and time, and surrendered to intimate communion with the Lord. These men are now recognized as **heroes of the faith because of what God did through them and in them.**

Anointing and prayer go together.

Dr. Richard Cecil said, "All the efforts of the minister shall be in vain if there is no anointing." The anointing should descend from the heavens and spread as perfume; giving taste, sensibility, form and shape to the ministry.

To prepare for ministry, the study of the Word and prayer should always have first place in a leader's life. In addition, all work should end with the Word of God and prayer.

The anointing is a conditional gift, established and increased, through the process in which it manifests itself. We must have an ardent desire to know God intimately, and to have steadfast prayer. These must be continually sought after, and longed for as a treasured gift. As we experience them, all other things will be considered as loss; once this happens, His power will begin to flow in our lives.

Where does the anointing originate?

The anointing comes directly from God as a response to prayer. Only those hearts, which are in constant prayer, may be full of His Holy Oil. The anointing can only be developed in praying lips. Continuous prayer is a price, which must be paid to increase the anointing in our lives.

John Wesley said: "Give me a hundred preachers who do not fear sin and who's only desire is for God, regardless of whether they are layman or clergy, because only they can establish the kingdom of heaven upon the earth, and make the doors of hell tremble."

The holier the man, the more he values prayer.

What should motivate us to pray?

The deep desire to:

❖ Have intimate communion with God

❖ Be used by Him

❖ Develop the anointing

❖ Hear and know His voice

❖ Help others to change and draw close to Him

Our heart's burning desire should be our motivating factor to pray. **Prayer and desire go hand in hand. Whatever the righteous desire, that is what they should receive.**

"24The fear of the wicked, it shall come upon him; but the desire of the righteous shall be granted."
Proverbs 10.24

We should all yearn to have intimacy with God; to see the Word of God and the anointing increase in our lives. When this becomes a true and fervent desire in us, we will find the strength and purpose to wake up early and pray.

As previously mentioned, the **longing for intimacy with God allows us to act and obtain the desires of our heart.**

Why are there people who neglect prayer as part of their lifestyle? The following reasons may explain why we do not have a constant life of prayer, perhaps it is because we need: discipline, commitment, perseverance, fasting and prayer.

1. **Lack of discipline.** Discipline is sacrifice, surrender, and self-denial. It also requires of us to have good habits and to put forth our best effort. We must discipline ourselves to pray daily. We should do this until prayer becomes part of our lifestyle. At times, we may be tired and unwilling to pray, but our disciplined lifestyle will allow us to submit to prayer.

110

2. **Lack of commitment**. Not making a firm decision to pray for prolonged periods of time, and choosing not to completely surrender unto the Lord, are reasons why we do not have prayer as part of our lifestyle. **The decision to pray must be accompanied by commitment and compromise.**

3. **Lack of perseverance.** Lack of perseverance is one of the greatest enemies a believer will face. If we do not persevere in prayer, we may begin to pray for a week or a few months and then give up.

3. **Fasting and prayer as part of our lifestyle**

   Fasting: To fast is to abstain from eating or drinking for a pre-determined period-of-time, with the objective of seeking God's face and to have a deep and intimate communion with Him.

   "12Yet even now," declares the Lord, "Return to me with all your heart, and with fasting, weeping and mourning..." Joel 2.12

The word 'return' here means to go back to the point of departure, to seek God's face. To return to God we must do it wholeheartedly, fasting and crying out to Him.

We are living perverted times. Children are rebellious and disrespectful, there is lack of integrity, sin is all around us and there is a breakdown of values. None of these things will change unless we seek God through our lifestyles of fasting and prayer.

"[16]And whenever you fast, do not put on a gloomy face as the hypocrites do, for they neglect their appearance in order to be seen fasting by men. Truly, I say to you they have their reward in full. [17]But you when you fast Anoint your head and wash your face so that you may not be seen fasting by men, [18]but by your Father who is in secret; and your Father who sees you in secret will repay you." Mathew 6.16-18

"[5]In stripes, in imprisonments, in tumults, in labor, in watchings, in fastings, [6]by purity, by knowledge, by long-suffering, by kindness, by the Holy Ghost, by love unfeigned." 2 Corinthians 6.5, 6

"[1]Now there were in the church at Antioch certain prophets and teachers: Barnabas, and Simeon who was called Niger, and Lucius of Cyrene, and Manaen who had been brought up with Herod the tetrarch, and Saul. [2]As they ministered to the Lord and fasted, the Holy Spirit said, "Set apart for Me Barnabas and Saul for the work to which I have called them." [3]And when they had fasted and prayed and laid their hands on them, they sent them away" Acts 13.1-3

It is important for us to implement "lifestyles of fasting and prayer." It may be done every week, twice a week, or every two months. It may be a partial, absolute or total fast; the choice is up to you, but commit to this "lifestyle".

We do not need to wait until we sense God directing us to fast and pray. Jesus said, *"When they fasted;"* this implies that we should decide when we should fast.

What are the three types of biblical fasting?

1. **Total fast.** This type of fast is done without eating any type of solid food or liquids, including water. Example: Esther and the Jewish people "did not eat nor drink."

2. **Absolute fast.** This type of fast is when solid foods are not eaten, but water may be taken.

   For example: *Matthew 4:1-1" and after having fasted forty days and forty nights, He was hungry."* Specifically, "no eating or drinking" was ever mentioned, and the Word does not mention that Jesus was thirsty during this time.

3. **Partial fast.** This type of fast is when certain types of foods and drinks are eliminated from our daily diet. One or two daily meals can be eliminated, such as breakfast and lunch or when only fruits or vegetables are eaten.

   "[3]I ate no pleasant bread, neither came flesh nor wine in my mouth, neither did I Anoint myself at all, till three whole weeks were fulfilled."
   Daniel 10.3

What is the purpose of fasting?

There are seven major reasons to fast and pray.

1. **To honor God.** When we fast, we honor God because we choose to separate ourselves to be with

Him; to seek His face; to dedicate our lives exclusively to Him; and to surrender and give Him the rightful place, which He richly deserves.

2. **To humble and repent before His presence.** We may not know that we are proud, just as we may not realize when we are humble. Arrogance and humility are mysteries. No one walks around confessing I am proud or I am humble. What we seem to be is what we are; this is a condition of the heart.

When we fast and pray God, will show us the condition of our heart.

"¹Now in the twenty and fourth day of this month the children of Israel were assembled with fasting and with sackcloth and earth upon them. ²And the seed of Israel separated themselves from all strangers, and stood and confessed their sins and the iniquities of their fathers." Nehemiah 9.1, 2

While we fast, God will show us any areas of pride we may have. He will humble us either privately or publicly. If He chooses to humble us publicly, our humiliation is prolonged because we resisted Him. However, if He chooses to humble us privately, the moment of humiliation will be shorter because we initiated it; we sought His face in submission and were willing to confront our shortcomings.

"¹⁵For thus said the high and lofty One who inhabited eternity, whose name is Holy: "I dwell in

the high and holy place with him also that is of a contrite and humble spirit, to revive the spirit of the humble and to revive the heart of the contrite ones." Isaiah 57.15

The Word of God teaches us that we should test ourselves, to see if we are standing in faith. How do we test ourselves? We do it in His presence, through fasting and prayer.

4. **To withstand any crisis.** Every time we undergo a crisis in our life, or if we are passing through deserts, temptations, financial problems, marital problems or any obstacle created by the enemy, it is time for fasting and prayer.

"[1] It came to pass after this also, that the children of Moab and the children of Ammon, and with them others besides the Ammonites, came against Jehoshaphat to battle. [2] Then there came some who told Jehoshaphat, saying, "There cometh a great multitude against thee from beyond the sea on this side of Syria; and behold, they are in Hazazontamar, which is Engedi." [3] And Jehoshaphat feared, and set himself to seek the LORD, and proclaimed a fast throughout all Judah." 2 Chronicles 20.1-3

When there is a mighty army surrounding us, we must confront it; or if we are experiencing a great crisis, it is time to fast. Every time we find ourselves facing a crisis in our lives, declare war against the enemy with fasting and prayer.

5. **To seek and hear God's direction.** Whenever we find ourselves in difficult situations, and unsure as to what to do next, do we: strike the rock, throw the rod, take authority, or wait on God. It is a time when we need to hear from Him. For this to happen, it is essential for us to implement fasting to our lifestyle.

"³He restored my soul; He leaded me in the paths of righteousness for His name's sake." Psalms 23.3

6. **To ordain someone into ministry.** Each time we are going to ordain someone into the ministry, we should fast. This is a very serious matter that should never be taken lightly, and which God deems very important.

"¹Now there were in the church at Antioch certain prophets and teachers: Barnabas, and Simeon who was called Niger, and Lucius of Cyrene, and Manaen who had been brought up with Herod the tetrarch, and Saul. ²As they ministered to the Lord and fasted, the Holy Spirit said, "Set apart for Me Barnabas and Saul for the work to which I have called them." ³And when they had fasted and prayed and laid their hands on them, they sent them away." Acts 13.1-3

7. **To develop spiritual sensitivity.** Fasting increases our sensitivity and spiritual perception. It enables us to understand areas of the Word that we were previously unable to grasp. When we have a difficult time hearing God's voice, we should fast in order to become sensitive to His voice.

Believers are not the only ones who fast. Witches, Satanists, and many other cults and religions have discovered the advantages of fasting. They all realize that their powers and strength are enhanced; and their abilities to communicate, and to channel spirits on their behalf is improved when they fast.

Many who have discovered the power of fasting are against the church of Christ. Can you imagine how much greater the power of God would be in our lives if we were to spend time fasting and praying?

8. **To loosen the bands of wickedness.** To "loosen" in Hebrew means to open a door that is closed; to release someone; to set a prisoner free; or to loosen the knot in a rope. Fasting and prayer are tools believers can use to destroy the traps and snares that the enemy brings into their lives. Fasting and prayer will open any doors, whether it is in business, work, marriage, health, etc.

"[6] Is not this the fast that I have chosen: to loose the bands of wickedness, to undo the heavy burdens, and to let the oppressed go free, and that ye break every yoke?" Isaiah 58.6

What are the steps to fasting?

1. **Declare a fast aloud before God.** Determine all the details of the fast and share them with the Lord. Tell God the type of fast you will be doing, whether it is partial, absolute or total. Also tell Him

for how long you will fast; when you will begin; and when you will end.

2. **Define the purpose of your fast.** What is the purpose of your fast? You may have more than one purpose for fasting. Before you begin to fast, specify the reason you are doing it. Example: "Lord, I declare this fast for the salvation of my children."

3. **Seek the help of the Holy Spirit.** He will console and comfort you, and keep you from becoming weak. Ask Him for spiritual, physical and emotional strength while you are fasting. This is an important point, since we are often tempted to shorten the fast when we begin to feel weak. If we seek the assistance of the Holy Spirit, He will give us the strength before hand.

4. **Receive the reward ahead of time.** Thank God beforehand for the outcome of that which you are fasting and praying for. Remember, **"You are not trying to buy God."** He rewards you, as He rewards those who diligently seek Him.

"⁴That thine almsgiving may be in secret; and thy Father who seethe in secret, Himself shall reward thee openly." Matthew 6.4

5. **Meditate and study the Word of God.** The study and meditation of the Word is a form of spiritual exercise that helps develop the anointing. The Lord told Joshua that he should study and meditate on

His Word. If we meditate on a particular thing, day and night, it is an indication that we are obsessed with that thing. God wants us to think on His Word day and night.

What does it mean to meditate on the Word?

To meditate is to: speak with oneself; to think out loud; to murmur; to direct spiritual attention; to speak through the heart; to create ideas of the heart; and to seek the spirit.

On what should we meditate?

We should meditate on God's law, all His wonders, and on our daily walk as believers.

"[12]I will meditate also on all of Thy work, and talk of Thy doings." Psalms 77.12

"[5]Now therefore, thus said the LORD of hosts: "Consider your ways! [6]Ye have sown much, and bring in little; ye eat, but ye have not nough; ye drink, but ye are not filled with drink; ye clothe yourselves, but there is none warm; and he that earnest wages, earnest wages to put it into a bag with holes." [7]Thus said the LORD of hosts: "Consider your ways! Haggai 1.5-7

Believers, who spend time meditating on the Word of God, know God intimately and have a greater anointing.

What do we accomplish when we meditate on the Word?

⇨ **Meditation edifies our spirit**. To meditate on the Word is for the spirit, as physical exercise is for the body; therefore, the spirit is further developed.

⇨ **Meditation allows you to take control over your mind.** When arguments, images, thoughts or ideas try to overtake us, we should meditate on His Word. Once we have control over our mind, we will be able to exercise greater authority over it. Meditating on the Word of God renews our mind as it removes old thoughts and replaces them with new ones.

"[14]Let the words of my mouth and the meditation of my heart be acceptable in Thy sight, O LORD, my Strength and my Redeemer" Psalms 19.14

⇨ **It provides greater understanding and revelation of the Word.** When we meditate on the Word of God, He enhances and reveals His Word in us.

"[5]Evil men understand not judgment, but they that seek the LORD understand all things". Proverbs 28.5

The fervent desire to be used by God.

This is another way to develop the anointing in our lives. We should all have a great passion to see the anointing increase in our lives.

"O God, Thou art my God; early will I seek Thee. My soul thirsted for Thee, my flesh longeth for Thee, in a dry and thirsty land where no water is, to see Thy power and Thy glory as I have seen Thee in the sanctuary." Psalm 63.1, 2

Every believer should have a deep desire to be used by God. His Word motivates us to seek the best gifts of the Spirit.

"Follow after charity, and desire spiritual gifts, but rather so that ye may prophesy." 1 Corinthians 14.1

The word "to seek" in Greek is "*zeloo*" meaning: ardent desire, a strong passion, and an instinct that motivates us beyond pride and the ability to reason.

When we desire to be used by the anointing of God, we cannot worry about what people think of us. God may lead us to do things that may damage our image or to do things that go beyond what is logical. God will also require of us to be bold and daring, and to do things others have never done before. This can only be possible when we are under the anointing. Then, we will see surprising results.

Unless we are willing to go beyond our intellectual reasoning, we will never be able to fully move under the anointing of God. Example: Jesus spat on the ground and used it when he healed the blind man.

Fear or shame may not allow us to obey the leading of the Spirit because of what others may think of us. For example: if God asked us to dance, would we do it regardless of what people may think of us?

What must we do to increase the anointing? We should have the instinctive desire to serve God. This should motivate us beyond reason and pride. Do not seek to understand everything before acting upon the leading of the Spirit. Just do what He wants, and do it by faith.

We conclude that there is no specific way to develop the anointing. However, it may be increased by: Anointed leaders; staying in Anointed ambiances; befriending Anointed men and women of God, by developing lifestyles of fasting and prayer and by having the strong desire to be used by God. These things increase the anointing in our lives.

CHAPTER 9

Ingredients of the Anointing

B elievers should desire to see the anointing develop in their lives. When we see someone operating under the anointing, it creates the desire within us to have that same anointing. We see Anointed leaders being used by God on the platform, but we do not see what went on behind the scenes; their preparation, dedication and sacrifice, before they got there.

God instructed the priests in the Old Testament to prepare the oil for the Holy anointing. They had to combine different types of oils together; each type of oil has a specific meaning and represents something in our lives. This will help us to understand how to increase the anointing in our lives.

"[22]Moreover the LORD spoke unto Moses, saying, [23]"Take thou also unto thee principal spices: of pure myrrh five hundred shekels, and of sweet cinnamon half as much (even two hundred and fifty shekels), and of sweet calamus two hundred and fifty shekels, [24]and of cassia five hundred shekels, according to the shekel of the sanctuary, and of olive oil a him. [25]And thou shall make from it an oil of holy ointment, an ointment compound according to the art of the perfumer; it shall be a holy anointing oil." Exodus 30.22-25

Each ingredient is unique in design. They each represent areas in our lives that God will deal with. The ingredients of the anointing are: myrrh, sweet cinnamon, sweet calamus, cassia and olive oil.

"[14]Now thanks be unto God, who always causeth us to triumph in Christ and who maketh manifest through us the savor of His knowledge in every place. [15]For we are unto God a sweet savor of Christ, in those who are saved and in those who perish."
2 Corinthians 2.14, 15

Myrrh, in Hebrew, means bitterness. This herb has a pleasing smell, but a bitter taste.

What does Myrrh represent? It represents the suffering and death of Christ. The wise men gave Jesus gold, incense and myrrh.

Gold represents the deity; incense represents prayers; and myrrh represents death.

What does gold mean to us? It means death of the old self. God will not pour His anointing upon us until we die to our old ego. We must die to our self, desires, preferences, etc...

How does God lead us to die to our ego? The process God uses is through "His dealing with us." This implies that we must go through deserts in our lives; storms, tribulations, trials, etc. **God's anointing enables us to die.**

126

Believers who desire to move under the anointing of the Holy Spirit must be willing to: die to self, deny their ego on a daily basis, always obey God, and even sacrifice their own personal desires.

"[3]And being in Bethany in the house of Simon the leper, as He sat at meat, there came a woman having an alabaster box of ointment of spikenard, very precious; and she broke the box and poured it on His head." Mark 14.3

Cinnamon- This spice represents firmness, stability and the gifts of the Holy Spirit. A believer's character is the foundation, which enables him to operate and sustain the anointing. Without a stable and firm foundation, the anointing will not flow. The person must also have a solid biblical foundation.

How can we apply these concepts to our lives? In order to have His anointing, we must develop Christ like characters. God must change a person internally before He uses the person externally. The apostle Paul taught us that the most effective way to move under the anointing is through love. Love is a gift and fruit of the Holy Spirit.

Cassia, in Hebrew, means to deny oneself; humble ourselves and to worship. Cassia is a plant with a strong odor.

What does Cassia represent? Cassia represents worship and humility before the Lord.

We must understand that the Lord expects us to worship Him before He pours out His anointing on us. In other words, to see the anointing manifested in our lives, we must be true worshipers.

"²³But the hour cometh and now is, when the true worshipers shall worship the Father in spirit and in truth; for the Father seeketh such to worship Him. ²⁴God is a Spirit, and they that worship Him must worship Him in spirit and in truth." John 4.23, 24

Calamus - The word calamus, in Hebrew, means rod. This red herb smells like ginger and grows along the riverbanks. The rod represents authority.

What does this mean to us? Calamus means that before God pours His anointing upon us and gives us authority, we must submit ourselves to authority. This is what the Word of God calls submission. Regardless of the calling in our life, we must submit and be accountable to someone.

Olive Oil - Olive oil represents God's dealings with us. The process of extracting oil from mature olives begins when the olives are placed in a cistern or heavy rocks. There the oil is extracted and the hard shell removed. The stone used in this process is called "gath shemen," which in Hebrew means Gethsemane, and translated it means oil churn.

The Word of God teaches us that Jesus was taken to Gethsemane to be poured out for us. This is the place where Jesus surrendered His Will for us. What does this mean to us? This represents that God processes our motivations as he deals with us. God takes us through Gethsemane for us to die to ourselves, to die to our will, and to purify our motivations.

This was part of an ancient process for pressing the olives. The hard shells were removed from the olives and the extracted oil was left in the cistern until the impurities were removed and the filth rose to the top. When we apply this concept to our lives, we see that God leads us through Gethsemane to be pressed until the hidden filth in our life rises to the surface. **God cleanses our motivations through this process**.

What does all this have to do with the anointing? God will purify our motives before He pours out His anointing. Let us remember that the purpose of the anointing is to serve and bless others, not to keep it for ourselves.

Now we will take the meaning of each ingredient and learn how to apply it to our lives.

Myrrh - represents death to ego, suffering, deserts, trials and the tribulations in our lives.

Cinnamon - represents the development of Jesus' character and the gifts of the Holy Spirit.

Cassia - represents worship and humility before God.

Calamus - represents authority. God demands that we submit to authority.

Olive Oil - represents God's dealings in our lives. When our ego is pressed, our motives are purified.

Once we have gone throughout these processes, the Holy Spirit Anoints us. God will not anoint us unless we are willing to undergo these difficult steps.

Before God can use us, we must be pure!

Reasons Why we Might Lose the Anointing

CHAPTER 10

Reasons Why
we Might Lose
the Anointing

God has anointed many people, but few are able to keep their anointing. There are several reasons why this may happen, but we will only mention the most common ones.

Why does an individual lose the anointing?

He loses his anointing because he did not separate himself for God. There are two Hebrew words meaning "to separate," these are: *Nazar and Khohodesh*. **One is based on works and the other on an established relationship with God.**

Nazar means to separate. (The word Nazarene originates here.) It is a visible example of separation. God separates someone from worldly things, external things, places he might have visited, etc.

Kohodesh means to separate for. This type of separa-ion produces holiness for God.

They lose their anointing because they separated themselves only from the visible things of this world (*nazar*). They probably did not **separate themselves for God** (*kohodesh*). This type of separation is the result of an intimate relationship with God. *Nazar* is a visible manifestation that does not produce holiness.

For instance: do not touch, do not drive, do not wear makeup, etc.

You are not sanctified when you separate yourself from evil things, **you are sanctified when you separate yourself for God, and it is at this point that you will begin to do what is right.**

What separates us for God?

- Our personal prayer time.
- Seeking His presence.
- Time in the Word.
- Intimate communion with Him.

Some have failed to recognize God's ways. Many Godly people understand God's power and His works, yet they do not understand His ways. The Word teaches us how God showed the Israelites His works and He showed Moses His ways. What are the ways of the Lord? They are the why's, how's and when's of whatever pleases Him. **God's ways are His heart's desire and His agenda.**

"[7]He made known His ways unto Moses, His acts unto the children of Israel." Psalms 103.7

When Paul offered sacrifices unto God is a good example of this. At that moment, God's ways were to draw him closer to Himself, not to win the battle.

What are the works of the Lord? They are God's manifested power, healing, deliverance, splitting the Red sea, etc. God has anointed many people, but unfortunately, most of them were more interested in knowing His works, rather than His ways. It is good to know His works, but God wants us to know His ways first. We are so accustomed to the magnificent, the spectacular, to see His gifts and abilities, that we neglect to get to know Him intimately. I believe that if we take the time to know God, He will immediately use us mightily in miracles, healings and other powerful ways.

Lack of humility will diminish the anointing. Humility goes beyond giving God the glory. True humbleness is keeping everything in its proper perspective. Certain things such as: acknowledging our own weaknesses produces humbleness in us and draws us closer to Him. Humility shows us that His ways are the best; though we may not fully understand them, it enables us to trust in Him and to become true worshipers. We should also recognize our absolute dependency upon Him.

What sets us apart for God? Our personal time of prayer, our search for Him, time spent studying the Word, and time spent in intimate communion with Him. These things separate us "for" God.

We must not compromise the Word. The enemy will try to tempt us so that we will compromise biblical principles.

135

"[15]Love not the world, neither the things that are in the world. If any man loves the world, the love of the Father is not in him. [16]For all that is in the world--the lust of the flesh, and the lust of the eyes, and the pride of life--is not of the Father, but is of the world."
1 John 2.15, 16

We must not abuse God's gift of the anointing. The anointing is not to be bought or sold; God does not anoint us for our personal use, nor for personal glory or for dishonest gain. We must be faithful stewards of God's anointing.

"[8]And thou shall take no bribe, for the bribe blindeth the wise and perverteth the words of the righteous."
Exodus 23.8

Great beginnings and sad endings.

In the Word we find several men who lost the anointing of God. These are some examples:

Gideon – He was a faithful, upright man when called by God; and God spoke well of him.

"[11]There came an angel of the LORD, and sat under an oak which was in Ophrah, that pertained unto Joash the Abiezrite; and his son Gideon threshed wheat by the wine press to hide it from the Midianites." Judges 6.11

Gideon's excuse:

"[15]And he said unto Him, "Oh my Lord, with what shall I save Israel? Behold, my family is poor in Manasseh, and I am the least in my father's house." Judges 6.15

God's mission for Gideon:

"[25]And it came to pass the same night, that the LORD said unto him, "Take thy father's young bullock, even the second bullock of seven years old, and throw down the altar of Baal that thy father hath, and cut down the Asherah pole that is by it;" Judges 6.25

Gideon's victory: He defeated an army of one hundred thousand men with only three hundred men. He remained humble and gave God the glory for the victory He had given him. He did not try to take God's place.

"[22]Then the men of Israel said unto Gideon, "Rule thou over us, both thou and thy son and thy son's son also; for thou hast delivered us from the hand of Midian." [23]And Gideon said unto them, "I will not rule over you, neither shall my son rule over you: the LORD shall rule over you." Judges 8.22, 23

Gideon's weakness: He destroyed his father's idols and built his own. He named his son Abimelec, meaning, "My father is King." He refused to lead the people in the beginning and later fell due to his lack of humility.

Samson – He had a supernatural birth, he was very strong and the Spirit of the Lord rested upon him.

"[24] And the woman bore a son, and called his name Samson; and the child grew, and the LORD blessed him." Judges 13.24

Samson's victory: He slaughtered a lion, broke chains and killed thirty men. In the beginning, God's powerful anointing was upon him.

Samson's fall: He refused his parents counsel and left with a philistine woman, Delilah. The reason for his fall was sexual sin.

"[15] And she said unto him, "How canst thou say, 'I love thee,' when thine heart is not with me? Thou hast mocked me these three times, and hast not told me wherein thy great strength lieth." Judges 16.15

Saul - He was humble, obedient and submissive unto the Lord in the beginning.

"[21] When he had caused the tribe of Benjamin to come near by their families, the family of Matri was taken, and Saul the son of Kish was taken; and when they sought him, he could not be found. [22] Therefore, they inquired of the LORD further if the man should yet come thither. And the LORD answered,

"Behold, he hath hid himself among the supplies."
1 Samuel 10.21, 22

Saul's fall: He lost his anointing because he made sacrifices before God and this was not part of his calling. He gave in to peer pressure, lacked patience for waiting on God, and he disobeyed and feared the enemy.

"[22] And Samuel said, "Hath the LORD as great delight in burnt offerings and sacrifices as in obeying the voice of the LORD? Behold, to obey is better than sacrifice, and to hearken than the fat of rams. [23] For rebellion is as the sin of witchcraft, and stubbornness is as iniquity and idolatry. Because thou hast rejected the word of the LORD, He hath also rejected thee from being king." [24] And Saul said unto Samuel, "I have sinned; for I have transgressed the commandment of the LORD and thy words, because I feared the people and obeyed their voice." 1 Samuel 15.22-24

Gehazi - Gehazi lost the anointing due to greed or his love of money. *2 Kings 5.1-27*

God's gifts and calling are irrevocable; they remain permanently within us throughout our lives. The anointing is not permanent, it is contingent, gradual, and temporary, and it can be lost if we neglect to behave properly. God used the men, previously mentioned, in mighty and powerful ways, but although their beginnings were great, the end of their lives was a sad ending. Initially they did separate themselves for

God, but failed to remain humble. They did not learn God's ways nor did they use their Gifts adequately, consequently, they lost their anointing.

To keep from falling we should have the fear of God in our hearts and seek to fulfill our God given calling. The final question would be: Can we lose the anointing? The answer to this question is yes we can lose it.

Let us ask God to strengthen us and to help us maintain pure motives, with the fear of the Lord in our hearts. Let us cherish all the blessings we receive from God, live in true humility, be in intimate communion with Him, and depend on Him more each day.

God has anointed each believer in different levels, some at higher levels than others. However, we must be determined to activate the anointing in our lives. We must continue to treasure it until it overflows, and to develop our character by dying to ourselves. Give God all the Glory and Honor, and serve Him by blessing others with His precious anointing.

How we can Receive a Mantle

CHAPTER 11

How we can Receive a Mantle

W e often hear of the Anointed mantles of Godly people in Christian charismatic circles. We should understand what an anointing mantle is and how we can have it.

What is a mantle?

Figuratively speaking, a mantle is a Godly representation of power and anointing over someone's life. In the Bible, a mantle is a robe worn over other clothes and used to protect the body from external elements; it is also called a cape. The common use of a mantle is to cover, to protect and to clothe.

Elijah and Elisha are biblical examples of how an individual receives the anointing mantle. Elisha asked for a double portion of Elijah's anointing and his petition was granted; as Elijah was leaving, he gave his mantle to Elisha.

How can we receive a mantle?

According to the Scriptures, there are different ways to receive a mantle. These are not the only ways, but we will study the most common found in the Bible.

When God directly imparts it. This happens when God directly anoints someone, as in the case of Jesus, where He does not use anyone else.

When does this happen? This is the anointing of a "precursor or a pioneer". God does things, never before seen, through people in new areas such as: miracles, signs and wonders.

An Anointed man will have the direct impartation from God. He receives the command to do things, never done before by other men, and to clear the way for others to follow.

We must keep in mind that these pioneers never had mentors to show them the way things needed to be done, God had to directly anoint them. God will usually use mentors to impart levels of anointing into our lives, but sometimes the mantle of anointing is directly imparted from God to man.

The "service towel" given to a godly person. Serving is the most common Biblical way to receive an anointing mantle. Although God can use whatever way He chooses to use, most of the time, He uses a mentor or a father figure to impart a mantle. The "service towel" to another person is one of them.

Let us take a look at a biblical example:

"[15]And the Lord said to him: 'Go, return on the way to the wilderness at Damascus, and when you have

arrived you shall Anoint Hazael, King over Aram."
1 Kings 19.15

Elijah had just decapitated the prophets of Baal, his enemies. When it rained, he realized that Jezebel was persecuting him and wanted to kill him; this discouraged him. It was at this point that God told him to go and anoint Hazael as king of Syria. God met him on the way and told him it was time for him to delegate and surrender his mantle to someone else because his time on earth was over. Elijah decided to give his mantle to Elisha, who received it as he was taken up by the tornado.

Let us see a couple of important issues in these verses.

"[19]So he departed thence, and found Elisha the son of Shaphat, who was plowing with the twelve yoke of oxen before him, and he with the twelthe: and Elijah passed by him, and cast his mantle upon him. [20]And he left the oxen, and ran after Elijah, and said, Let me I pary kiss my father and my mother, and then I will follow thee. And he said unto him, go back again: for what have I done to thee? [21]And he returned back from him, and took a yoke of oxen and slew them, and boiled their flesh with the instruments of the oxen and they did eat. Then he arose, and went after Elijah, and ministered unto him." 1 Kings 19.19-21

"Elisha, the son of Shaphat, was plowing with the twelve yoke of oxen." This leads us to think that God will not anoint someone who is idle.

God gives the mantle to those that are busy serving Him. Unless you are busy serving God, do not expect to receive the mantle.

"Elisha followed Elijah everywhere." Some people are anointed, but when their time comes, they choose worldly things to keep them busy. Here we see that Elisha was not satisfied with the level of anointing that he had and he desired a higher level of it. He prayed that God would anoint him with a greater level of the anointing, and as he waited, he kept busy serving the Lord. Elisha's obedience was unconditional; as a result, he received his mantle.

"He went back, took a pair of bulls and slaughtered them." Elisha wanted to be certain he was not coming back, so he rejoiced with the people the fact that he had received what he had waited so long for; and to make sure of this, he celebrated with the people, and gave them everything he owned, making sure there was nothing left for him to come back to.

"He got up, and went behind Elijah and served him." Service is the key. In order for Elisha to receive the mantle that was over Elijah's life, he had to serve him. Historians believe that Elisha put on the "towel of service" and served Elijah, the man of God, for thirty years.

What examples of service would we see from Elisha if he were serving Elijah today? I assume he would carry his clothes, wash his feet, carry his luggage, and pray for him if he felt down.

He would carry his water and his Bible, dry his sweat as he ministered, and drive his car. He would be with him during good times as well as the bad times. He would see God's power manifested through him, plus so many other things we cannot even mention right now.

Elisha served God for thirty years, through his service to Elijah, but when God wanted to take Elijah up in the whirlwind, he asked Elisha to stay back and not follow him.

"¹And it came to pass, when the Lord would take up Elijah into heaven by a whirlwind, that Elijah went with Elisha from Gilgal. ²And Elijah said unto Elisha, Tarry here, I pray thee; for the Lord hath sent me to Bethel. And Elisha said unto him , As the Lord liveth, and as thy soul liveth, I will not leave thee. So they went down to Bethel." 2 Kings 2.1, 2

Elisha answered with the Jewish expression, **"Jehovah lives and your soul lives, I shall not leave you."** What he meant to say with this expression was that as long as the anointing was upon him, and until he received his own anointing, he was not going to leave him.

Elijah tried to separate himself from Elisha on four separate occasions (He wanted to go to Gilgal, Bethel, Jericho and Jordan), but four times Elisha refused saying, "No, I will remain with you."

"⁹And it came to pass, when they were gone over, that Elijah said to Elisha, Ask what I shall do for thee, before I be taken away from thee. And Elisha said I pray thee, let a double portion of thy spirit be upon me." 2 Kings 2.9

Elisha did not ask for land, riches or fame. He asked for the anointing for which he had longed and prayed for during thirty years. **"I beg that you leave me a double portion of your spirit."** We can see that he was not asking for a double portion of the Holy Spirit, he was asking for a double portion of Elijah's spirit.

What does this mean? It means that Elijah had accumulated in his spirit, the anointing he had received throughout the years. At the same time, he gained knowledge, wisdom, revelation, power, authority and sanctity. Eventually, he was ready to impart all that he had accumulated; and when Elisha asked Elijah for the double portion of his spirit, he was ready to give it.

There is an important concept here. In order for someone to impart a spiritual condition to someone else, he must have accumulated it himself in his own spirit. It is noteworthy to know that anointed, godly people can pray for us, and lay hands on us, so that we can receive God's anointing. However, unless we serve them for a long time, they cannot impart their mantle on us. **The person who has the anointing mantle is the only one that can impart it; he can transfer it to another anointed person who serves him directly.**

There are many Godly people, whom God has yet to take to be with Him, because they have not found other people to whom they can transfer their mantle.

Our generation has lost the 'towel of service' mantle. This may be another reason why the mantle is not transferred. My advice to you as a believer, a pastor, an evangelist, a teacher, an apostle or a prophet is: serve your leader or pastor, carry his Bible, drive his car, and serve any way you can. Simply put on your 'towel of service' and serve.

"¹⁰And he said, Thou has asked a hard thing: never-theless, if thou see me when I am taken from thee, it shall be so unto thee; but if not, it shall not be so."
2 Kings 2.10

We must constantly pay a high price for the anointing; it is conditional, temporary, and it cannot be imparted to just anyone, unless he has paid the price. When we learn to pay the price, God will anoint us.

Elisha's long awaited moment finally arrived im-mediately after they spoke. I can just picture Elisha re-membering the years he served Elijah.

"¹¹And it came to pass, as they still went on and talked, that, behold, there appeared a chariot of fire, and horses of fire, and parted them both asunder; and Elijah went up by a whirlwind into heaven. ¹²And Elisha saw it, and he cried, My father, my father, the chariot of Israel and the horsemen thereof. And he

saw him no more: and he took hold of his own clothes, and rent them in to pieces." 2 Kings 2.11, 12

When Elisha received Elijah's mantle, I imagine him saying as he cried, "The decision I made to follow and serve this man, the times he disciplined me, the times I was criticized and judged together with him, were worth it. The things I left behind to follow him, things like my land, my cattle, and my properties, these too were worth giving up. The lonely moments spent by his side, the waiting and the sleepless night, these too were worth it. All of these were worth going through and giving up for this mantle I have just received." There is nothing in the world that can compare to the wonderful anointing of the Holy Spirit.

"13He took up also the mantle of Elijah that fell from him, and went back and stood by the bank of Jordan: 14And he took the mantle of Elijah that fell from him, and smothe the waters, and said: Where is the Lord God of Elijah? And when he also had smiten the waters, they parted hither and tither; and Elisha went over. 15And when the sons of the prophets which were to view at Jericho saw him, they said, the spirit of Elijah, doth rest on Elisha. And they came to meet him and bowed themselves to the ground before him." 2 Kings 2.13-15

The final test. Did he really receive the double portion of the anointing? Well, he threw the mantle in the Jordan River and the waters split in two. At that instant, he realized he had received the double anointing.

Notice that when Elisha requested the anointing he said, "My father." Elisha and Elijah had a father-son relationship. I believe that only those that feel fatherly love can transfer the mantle of anointing. Very few Godly men are able to multiply themselves. Many of them lack fatherly love. Others are not interested in having anyone else do what they are doing; one reason for this may be that they are insecure of their mantle.

What was the result? Elisha received Elijah's mantle. He served Elijah as a friend, mentor and father. During his lifetime, Elijah realized eight miracles, and Elisha realized fifteen miracles while he was alive and one after he was dead. Scripture tells us that his dry dead bones raised someone from the death, thus ending the double portion of his anointing. In total, Elisha participated in sixteen miracles.

"[21]And it came to pass, as they were burying a man, that behold, they spied a band of men: *and they cast the man into the sepulcher of Elisha: and when the man was let down, and touched the bones of Elisha, he revived, and stood up on his feet." 2 Kings 13.21*

If we want the anointing mantle, we need to draw near to an Anointed, Godly person and serve him. When our time comes, we will receive our own anointing. Remember, when we serve Godly people, we are ultimately, serving the anointing mantle that rests upon them.

There are other biblical examples of mantles that were imparted. We see it in the cases of Moses with Joshua and Jesus with his disciples. The most common manner of receiving a mantle, as described in the Bible, is through the laying on of hands. Let us look at this scripture:

"⁹And Joshua the son of Nun was full of the spirit of wisdom; for Moses had laid his hands upon him: and the children of Israel hearkened unto him, and did as the Lord commanded Moses." Deuteronomy 34.9

A mantle can be received in several ways:

1. **Directly from God.** When God wants to do something yet to be done, He will impart a mantle on the person of His choosing. In the absence of an earthly father to disciple us, we must learn directly from the Lord. In other words, God will impart a direct anointing upon our life, without the need for a mentor, when pioneer work needs to be done.

2. **From the Godly person we serve.** When we serve a Godly person, and our time comes to receive our own anointing, God will usually do it in the same way that He Anointed the person we are serving.

Are there any other ways that God imparts His mantle? Yes there are, however, the most common way mentioned in the Bible is by serving God and remaining in Anointed environments.

152

Conclusion

S ome principles in this book are the result of my years in ministry, profound biblical studies and my intimate relationship with God. I pray that reading this book has touched your life, and I hope you have been challenged to penetrate into deeper realms of the anointing by intensifying your daily walk with God.

Remember, without the Holy Spirit's anointing we are unable to obtain great results in our ministries. The anointing does not come automatically or with time. It comes only after God takes us through, and completes in us, the process of self-denial, for the purpose of developing Christ's character in us. During this process, God will use methods difficult to comprehend, but of His own design, so that we may be able to advance into other dimensions where He will manifest his supernatural ways from a different perspective.

To mention only a few, the major keys for increasing the anointing are: obedience, service and humility. We must serve God by serving the people He has put over us. We must never forget that the anointing is not for our personal Glory, but to Glorify Jesus.

In His established time, you too, will receive your mantle of anointing.

Bibliography

Biblia Plenitud, Caribe Editorial, Reina Valera: Miami, Florida, 1960.

Damazio, Frank. *The Making of a Leader*. Editorial BT Publishing: Portland, Oregon, ISBN: 0-914936-84-0, 1988, pp. 284-286, 291, 293, 303.

Diccionario Expositivo de las Palabras del Antiguo Testamento y Nuevo Testamento. Caribe Editorial, Inc,/Division Thomas Nelson, Inc: Nashville, Tennes-see, ISBN: 0-89922-495-4, 1999, pp. 333, 558, 925, 926.

Dictionary Spanish to English, English to Spanish. Editorial Larousse S.A., printed in Dinamarca, Num. 81, Mexico, ISBN: 2-03-420200-7, ISBN: 70-607-371-X, 1993, pp. 687-688.

Dollar, Creflo A. Jr. *Understanding God's Purpose for the Anointing*. Editorial and Creative Service: Edmond Oklahoma, ISBN: 0-9634781-0-9, 1992, pp. 52, 31.

Hagin, Kenneth E. *Understand the Anointing*. Editorial Faith Library, Kenneth Hagin Ministries, Tulsa, Oklahoma, ISBN: 0-89275-507-0, 1983, pp. 11, 37, 78, 119, 149.

Maxwell, John. *Desarrolle el Líder que esta en Usted.* Betania Editorial, Caribe Editorial: Nashville, Tennessee ISBN: 0-88113-293-4, 1996, pp. 51, 13, 169.

Munroe, Myles. *Becoming a Leader.* Pneuma Editorial Life Publishing: Bakersfield, California, ISBN: 1-56229-401-6, 1993, pp. 155, 156, 159, 160.

Packer, JI, M.C. Tenney Editors. *Illustrated Manners and Customs of The Bible.* Caribe Editorial: Nashville, Tennessee ISBN: 0-7852-1231-0, 1980, pp. 246, 319.

Sanders, Oswald J. *Liderazgo Espiritual,* Portavoz/filial Editorial of kregil Publications: Grand Rapid, Michigan, ISBN: 0-8254-1650-7, 1995, pp. 119, 155.

Ward, Lock A. Nuevo Diccionario de la Biblia. Unilit Editorial: Miami, Florida, ISBN: 0-7899-0217-6, 1999, pp. 1,040.

BOOKS BY
GUILLERMO MALDONADO

Ascending in Prayer and Worship and Descending in War
A Biblical Foundation for New Believers
Dangers of Unforgiveness
Deliverance, the Children's Bread
Forgiveness
Discover your Purpose and Calling in God
Hope in Times of Crisis
How to Fast Effectively
How to Hear the Voice of God
How to Return to Our First Love
How to Walk in the Supernatural Power of God
Inner Healing and Deliverance
Jesus Heals your Sickness Today
Leaders that Conquer
Overcoming Depression
Overcoming Fear
Overcoming Pride
Prayer
The Family
The Glory of God
The Holy Anointing
The Kingdom of God and its Righteousness
The Kingdom of Power: How to Demonstrate It Here and Now
The Ministry of the Apostle
The New Wine Generation

BOOKS BY
GUILLERMO MALDONADO

To see our complete catalogue, in English and in Spanish, to find
a local bookstore near you, or to purchase directly from the
publisher, please contact us at: sales@erjpub.org
www.erjpub.org

ERJ Publicaciones
13651 SW 143 Ct. #101
Miami, FL 33186
(305) 382-3171